Alexander Roberts, James Sir Donaldson

Ante-Nicene Christian Library

Translations of the writings of the fathers down to A.D. 325.

Alexander Roberts, James Sir Donaldson

Ante-Nicene Christian Library
Translations of the writings of the fathers down to A.D. 325.

ISBN/EAN: 9783742854582

Manufactured in Europe, USA, Canada, Australia, Japa

Cover: Foto ©Andreas Hilbeck / pixelio.de

Manufactured and distributed by brebook publishing software (www.brebook.com)

Alexander Roberts, James Sir Donaldson

Ante-Nicene Christian Library

NOTICE TO SUBSCRIBERS.

MESSRS. CLARK have now the very great pleasure of publishing the final issue of the Ante-Nicene Series:—

THE COMPLETION OF ORIGEN AGAINST CELSUS; and

EARLY LITURGIES; with Fragments not hitherto given.

They are thankful for the support they have received in a very arduous undertaking; and they take this opportunity of acknowledging the great services of the Editors, whose learning has recommended the Series to Scholars, whilst their fairness and impartiality have been admitted by men of all shades of opinion.

An Index Volume to the whole Series is in active preparation, and will be a most useful addition to its value. It will be published at a very moderate price, and it is particularly requested that those who desire it will send their names as soon as possible to the Publishers.

Messrs. CLARK regret that they have received very little encouragement to publish the HOMILIES OF ORIGEN; but they are still open to the consideration of the matter if sufficient support can be obtained.

They trust that the Subscribers to the Ante-Nicene Series will continue their subscription to the WORKS OF ST. AUGUSTINE, of which four volumes are now ready, viz.:—

THE CITY OF GOD. In Two Volumes.

WRITINGS IN CONNECTION WITH THE DONATIST CONTROVERSY. One Volume.

THE ANTI-PELAGIAN WRITINGS OF AUGUSTINE. Vol. I.

They are glad to announce as in contemplation a uniform translation of the WORKS OF CHRYSOSTOM.

ANTE-NICENE

CHRISTIAN LIBRARY:

TRANSLATIONS OF
THE WRITINGS OF THE FATHERS
DOWN TO A.D. 325.

EDITED BY THE
REV. ALEXANDER ROBERTS, D.D.,
AND
JAMES DONALDSON, LL.D.

VOL. XXIV.

EARLY LITURGIES AND OTHER DOCUMENTS.

EDINBURGH:
T. & T. CLARK, 38, GEORGE STREET.
MDCCCLXXII.

PRINTED BY MURRAY AND GIBB,
FOR
T. & T. CLARK, EDINBURGH.

LONDON, ... HAMILTON, ADAMS, AND CO.
DUBLIN, ... JOHN ROBERTSON AND CO.
NEW YORK, . . . C. SCRIBNER AND CO.

LITURGIES

AND OTHER DOCUMENTS

OF THE

ANTE-NICENE PERIOD.

EDINBURGH:
T. & T. CLARK, 38, GEORGE STREET.
MDCCCLXXII

THE Liturgy of St. James has been translated by WILLIAM MACDONALD, M.A.; that of the Evangelist Mark by GEORGE ROSS MERRY, B.A.; and that of the Holy Apostles by DR. DONALDSON.

CONTENTS.

EARLY LITURGIES.

	PAGE
INTRODUCTORY NOTICE, ...	3
I. THE DIVINE LITURGY OF JAMES, ...	11
II. THE DIVINE LITURGY OF THE HOLY APOSTLE AND EVANGELIST MARK, ...	47
III. LITURGY OF THE HOLY APOSTLES, OR ORDER OF THE SACRAMENTS, ...	73
The Liturgy of the Blessed Apostles, composed by St. Adæus and St. Maris, Teachers of the Easterns, . . .	77

SYRIAC DOCUMENTS OF THE ANTE-NICENE PERIOD.

INTRODUCTORY NOTICE, ...	95
AMBROSE, ...	97
A LETTER OF MARA, SON OF SERAPION, . . .	105

SELECTIONS FROM THE PROPHETIC SCRIPTURES, . 117

FRAGMENTS OF CLEMENS ALEXANDRINUS.

I. FROM THE LATIN TRANSLATION OF CASSIODORUS, . . .	139
1. Comments on the First Epistle of Peter, . . .	139
2. Comments on the Epistle of Jude, ...	143
3. Comments on the First Epistle of John, . . .	147
4. Comments on the Second Epistle of John, . . .	153
II. FROM NICETAS BISHOP OF HERACLEA'S CATENA, . .	154
III. FROM THE CATENA ON LUKE, EDITED BY CORDERIUS, . .	157

		PAGE
IV.	From the Books of the Hypotyposes,	158
V.	From the Book on Providence,	162
VI.	From the Book "On the Soul,"	163
VII.	From the Book "On Slander,"	164
VIII.	Other Fragments from Antonius Melissa,	164
IX.	Fragment of the Treatise on Marriage,	166
X.	Fragments of other Lost Books,	166
XI.	Fragments found in Greek only in the Oxford Edition,	167
XII.	Fragments not given in the Oxford Edition,	175

EARLY LITURGIES.

INTRODUCTORY NOTICE.

HE word "Liturgy" has a special meaning as applied to the following documents. It denotes the service used in the celebration of the Eucharist.

Various liturgies have come down to us from antiquity; and their age, authorship, and genuineness have been matter of keen discussion. In our own country two writers on this subject stand specially prominent: the Rev. William Palmer, M.A., who in his *Origines Liturgicæ* (Oxford, 1832) gave a dissertation on Primitive Liturgies; and the Rev. J. Mason Neale, who devoted a large portion of his life to liturgies, edited four of them in his *Tetralogia Liturgica* (London, 1849), five of them in his *Liturgies of St. Mark, St. James, St. Clement, St. Chrysostom, and St. Basil* (sec. ed. London, 1868), and discussed them in a masterly manner in several works, but especially in his *General Introduction to a History of the Holy Eastern Church* (London, 1850).

Ancient liturgies are generally divided into four families, —the Liturgy of the Jerusalem Church, adopted throughout the East; the Alexandrian, used in Egypt and the neighbouring countries; and the Roman and Gallican Liturgies. To these Neale has added a fifth, the Liturgy of Persia or Edessa.

There is also a liturgy not included in any of these families—the Clementine. It seems never to have been used in any public service. It forms part of the eighth book of the *Apostolical Constitutions* (Ante-Nicene Christian Library, vol. xvii.).

The age ascribed to these documents depends very much

on the temperament and inclination of the inquirer. Those who have great reverence for them think that they must have had an apostolic origin, that they contain the apostolic form, first handed down by tradition, and then committed to writing, but they allow that there is a certain amount of interpolation and addition of a date later than the Nicene Council. Such words as "consubstantial" and "mother of God" bear indisputable witness to this. Others think that there is no real historical proof of their early existence at all, —that they all belong to a late date, and bear evident marks of having been written long after the age of the apostles.

There can scarcely be a doubt that they were not committed to writing till a comparatively late day. Those who think that their origin was apostolic allow this. "The period," says Palmer,[1] "when liturgies were first committed to writing is uncertain, and has been the subject of some controversy. Le Brun contends that no liturgy was written till the fifth century; but his arguments seem quite insufficient to prove this, and he is accordingly opposed by Muratori and other eminent ritualists. It seems certain, on the other hand, that the liturgy of the *Apostolical Constitutions* was written at the end of the third or beginning of the fourth century; and there is no reason to deny that others may have been written about the same time, or not long after."

Neale[2] sums up the results of his study in the following words: "I shall content myself therefore with assuming, (1) that these liturgies, though not composed by the Apostles whose names they bear, were the legitimate developement of their unwritten tradition respecting the Christian Sacrifice; the words, probably, in the most important parts, the general tenor in all portions, descending unchanged from the apostolic authors. (2) That the Liturgy of S. James is of earlier date, as to its main fabric, than A.D. 200; that the Clementine Office is at least not later than 260; that the Liturgy of S.

[1] *Origines Liturgicæ*, p. 11.
[2] *General Introduction to the History of the Holy Eastern Church*, p. 319.

Mark is nearly coeval with that of S. James; while those of S. Basil and S. Chrysostom are to be referred respectively to the Saints by whom they purport to be composed. In all these cases, several manifest insertions and additions do not alter the truth of the general statement."

1. The Roman Liturgy. The first writer who is supposed to allude to a Roman Liturgy is Innocentius, in the beginning of the fifth century; but it may well be doubted whether his words refer to any liturgy now extant. Some have attributed the authorship of the Roman Liturgy to Leo the Great, who was made bishop of Rome in A.D. 451; some to Gelasius, who was made bishop of Rome in A.D. 492; and some to Gregory the First, who was made bishop of Rome in A.D. 590. Such being the opinions of those who have given most study to the subject, we have not deemed it necessary to translate it, though Probst, in his *Liturgie der drei ersten christlichen Jahrhunderte* (Tübingen, 1870), probably out of affection for his own Church, has given it a place beside the Clementine and those of St. James and St. Mark.

2. The Gallican has still less claim to antiquity. In fact, Daniel marks it among the spurious ($νόθοι$).[1] Mabillon tries to prove that three ecclesiastics had a share in the authorship of this liturgy: Musæus, presbyter of Marseilles, who died after the middle of the fifth century; Sidonius, bishop of Auvergne, who died A.D. 494; and Hilary, bishop of Poictiers, who died A.D. 366.[2] Palmer strives to show with great ingenuity that it is not improbable that the Gallican Liturgy may have been originally derived from St. John; but his arguments are merely conjectures.

3. The Liturgy of St. James, the Liturgy of the Church of Jerusalem. Asseman, Zaccaria, Dr. Brett, Palmer, Trollope, and Neale, think that the main structure of this liturgy is the work of St. James, while they admit that it contains some evident interpolations. Leo Allatius, Bona, Bellarmine, Baronius, and some others, think that the whole is

[1] *Codex Liturgicus*, vol. iv. p. 35, note.
[2] Palmer, vol. i. p. 144.

the genuine production of the apostle. Cave, Fabricius, Dupin, Le Nourry, Basnage, Tillemont, and many others, think that it is entirely destitute of any claim to an apostolic origin, and that it belongs to a much later age.

"From the Liturgy of S. James," says Neale, "are derived, on the one hand, the forty Syro-Jacobite offices: on the other, the Cæsarean office, or Liturgy of S. Basil, with its offshoots; that of S. Chrysostom, and the Armeno-Gregorian."[1]

There are only two manuscripts of the Greek Liturgy of St. James,—one of the tenth, the other of the twelfth century, —with fragments of a third. The first edition appeared at Rome in 1526. In more recent times it has been edited by Rev. W. Trollope, M.A. (Edinburgh, T. & T. Clark, 1848), Neale in the two works mentioned above, and Daniel in his *Codex Liturgicus*. Bishop Rattray edited the *Anaphora* (London, 1744), and attempted to separate the original from the interpolations, "though," says Neale, "the supposed restoration is unsatisfactory enough." Bunsen, in his *Analecta Ante-Nicæna*, vol. iii., has tried to restore the *Anaphora* to the state in which it may have been in the fourth century, "as far as was possible—*quantum fieri potuit*."

4. The Liturgy of St. Mark, the liturgy of the church of Alexandria. The same difference of opinion exists in regard to the age and genuineness of this liturgy as we found existing in regard to that of St. James, and the same scholars occupy the same relative position.

The offshoots from St. Mark's Liturgy are St. Basil, St. Cyril, and St. Gregory, and the Ethiopic Canon or Liturgy of All Apostles. In regard to the Liturgy of St. Cyril, Neale says that it is "to all intents and purposes the same as that of S. Mark; and it seems highly probable that the Liturgy of S. Mark came, as we have it now, from the hands of S. Cyril, or, to use the expression of Abu'lberkat, that Cyril 'perfected' it."[2]

There is only one manuscript of the Liturgy of St. Mark, probably belonging to the twelfth century. The first edition

[1] *General Introd.* p. 317.   [2] *Ibid.* p. 324.

appeared at Paris in 1583. The liturgy is given in Renaudot's *Liturgiarum Orientalium Collectio*, tom. i. pp. 120–148 (editio secunda correctior. Francofurti ad Moenum, 1847), in Neale's two works, and in Daniel's *Codex Liturgicus*.

5. The Liturgy of the Apostles Adæus and Maris. This liturgy has been brought prominently forward by Neale, who says: "It is generally passed over as of very inferior importance, and Renaudot alone seems to have been prepared to acknowledge in some degree its great antiquity."[1] He thinks that it is "one of the earliest, and perhaps the very earliest, of the many formularies of the Christian Sacrifice."[2] It is one of the three Nestorian liturgies, the other two being that of Nestorius and that of Theodore the interpreter.

A Latin translation of it is given in Renaudot's *Collectio* (tom. ii. pp. 578–592, ed. sec.), which is reprinted in Daniel's *Codex Liturgicus*. It is from this version that our translation is made. Several prayers and hymns are indicated only by the initial words, and the rubrical directions are probably of a much later date than the text.

The Liturgies are divided into two parts,—the part before "Lift we up our hearts," and the part after this. The first is termed the Proanaphoral Part, the second the Anaphora.

Trollope describes what he conceives to be the form of worship in the early Church, thus:[3] "The service of this day divided itself into two parts; at the latter of which, called in the Eastern Churches *Liturgia mystica*, and in the Western *Missa fidelium*, none but perfect and approved Christians were allowed to be present. To the *Missa Catechumenorum*, or that part of the service which preceded the prayers peculiar to communicants only, not only believers, but Gentiles, were admitted, in the hope that some might possibly become converts to the faith. After the Psalms and Lessons with which the service commenced, as on ordinary occasions, a section from the Acts of the Apostles or the Epistles was read; after which the deacon or presbyter read the Gospel. Then followed an exhortation from

[1] *General Introd.* p. 319.   [2] *Ibid.* p. 323.   [3] *Introduction*, p. 11.

one or more of the presbyters; and the bishop or president delivered a *Homily* or *Sermon*, explanatory, it should seem, of the Scripture which had been read, and exciting the people to an imitation of the virtues therein exemplified. When the preacher had concluded his discourse with a doxology in praise of the Holy Trinity, a deacon made proclamation for all infidels and non-communicants to withdraw; then came the dismissal of the several classes of catechumens, energumens, competents, and penitents, after the prayers for each respectively, as on ordinary days; and the *Missa fidelium* commenced. This office consisted of two parts, essentially distinct: viz., of *prayers for the faithful*, and for mankind in general, introductory to the Oblation; and the *Anaphora* or *Oblation* itself. The introductory part varied considerably in the formularies of different churches; but in the *Anaphora* all the existing liturgies so closely agree, in substance at least, if not in words, that they can only be reasonably referred to the same common origin. Their arrangement, indeed, is not always the same; but the following essential points belong, without exception, to them all:—1. The Kiss of Peace; 2. The form beginning, *Lift up your hearts*; 3. The Hymn, *Therefore with angels*, etc.; 4. Commemoration of the words of Institution; 5. The Oblation; 6. Prayer of Consecration; 7. Prayers for the Church on Earth; 8. Prayers for the Dead; 9. The Lord's Prayer; 10. Breaking of the Bread; 11. Communion."

Neale gives a more minute account of the different parts of the service. He divides the proanaphoral portion into parts in the following manner:[1]

"1. The Mass of the Catechumens.
- I. The Preparatory Prayers.
- II. The Initial Hymn or Introit.
- III. The Little Entrance.
- IV. The Trisagion.
- V. The Lections.
- VI. The Prayers after the Gospel, and expulsion of the Catechumens.

---

[1] *General Introduction*, p. 359.

"2. The Mass of the Faithful
- I. The Prayers for the Faithful.
- II. The Great Entrance.
- III. The Offertory.
- IV. The Kiss of Peace.
- V. The Creed.

The anaphora he divides into four parts in the following manner:[1]

"The great Eucharistic Prayer.
- I. The Preface.
- II. The Prayer of the Triumphal Hymn.
- III. The Triumphal Hymn.
- IV. Commemoration of our Lord's Life.
- V. Commemoration of Institution.

"The Consecration.
- VI. Words of Institution of the Bread.
- VII. Words of Institution of the Wine.
- VIII. Oblation of the Body and Blood.
- IX. Introductory Prayer for the Descent of the Holy Ghost.
- X. Prayer for the Change of Elements.

"The great Intercessory Prayer.
- XI. General Intercession for Quick and Dead.
- XII. Prayer before the Lord's Prayer.
- XIII. The Lord's Prayer.
- XIV. The Embolismus.

"The Communion.
- XV. The Prayer of Inclination.
- XVI. The 'Holy Things for Holy Persons,' and Elevation of the Host.
- XVII. The Fraction.
- XVIII. The Confession.
- XIX. The Communion.
- XX. The Antidoron: and Prayers of Thanksgiving."

The whole subject is discussed by Mr. Neale with extraordinary minuteness, fulness of detail, and perfect mastery of his subject; and to his work we refer those who wish to prosecute the study of the subject.

[1] *General Introduction*, p. 463.

THE DIVINE LITURGY OF JAMES,

THE HOLY APOSTLE AND BROTHER OF THE LORD.

The Priest.

SOVEREIGN Lord our God, contemn me not, defiled with a multitude of sins: for, behold, I have come to this Thy divine and heavenly mystery, not as being worthy; but looking only to Thy goodness, I direct my voice to Thee: God be merciful to me, a sinner; I have sinned against Heaven, and before Thee, and am unworthy to come into the presence of this Thy holy and spiritual table, upon which Thy only-begotten Son, and our Lord Jesus Christ, is mystically set forth as a sacrifice for me, a sinner, and stained with every spot. Wherefore I present to Thee this supplication and thanksgiving, that Thy Spirit the Comforter may be sent down upon me, strengthening and fitting me for this service; and count me worthy to make known without condemnation the word, delivered from Thee by me to the people, in Christ Jesus our Lord, with whom Thou art blessed, together with Thy all-holy, and good, and quickening, and consubstantial Spirit, now and ever, and to all eternity. Amen.

Prayer of the standing beside the altar.

II. Glory to the Father, and to the Son, and to the Holy Spirit, the triune light of the Godhead, which is unity subsisting in trinity, divided, yet indivisible: for the Trinity is the one God Almighty, whose glory the heavens declare, and the earth His dominion, and the sea His might, and every sentient and intellectual creature at all times proclaims His majesty: for all glory becomes Him, and honour and might, greatness and magnificence, now and ever, and to all eternity. Amen.

Prayer of the incense at the beginning.

III. Sovereign Lord Jesus Christ, O Word of God, who didst freely offer Thyself a blameless sacrifice upon the cross to God even the Father, the coal of double nature, that didst touch the lips of the prophet with the tongs, and didst take away his sins, touch also the hearts of us sinners, and purify us from every stain, and present us holy beside Thy holy altar, that we may offer Thee a sacrifice of praise: and accept from us, Thy unprofitable servants, this incense as an odour of a sweet smell, and make fragrant the evil odour of our soul and body, and purify us with the sanctifying power of Thy all-holy Spirit: for Thou alone art holy, who sanctifiest, and art communicated to the faithful; and glory becomes Thee, with Thy eternal Father, and Thy all-holy, and good, and quickening Spirit, now and ever, and to all eternity. Amen.

Prayer of the commencement.

IV. O beneficent King eternal, and Creator of the universe, receive Thy church, coming unto Thee through Thy Christ: fulfil to each what is profitable; lead all to perfection, and make us perfectly worthy of the grace of Thy sanctification, gathering us together within Thy holy church, which Thou hast purchased by the precious blood of Thy only-begotten Son, and our Lord and Saviour Jesus Christ, with whom Thou art blessed and glorified, together with Thy all-holy, and good, and quickening Spirit, now and ever, and to all eternity. Amen.

The Deacon.

V. Let us again pray to the Lord.

The Priest, prayer of the incense at the entrance of the congregation.

God, who didst accept the gifts of Abel, the sacrifice of Noah and of Abram, the incense of Aaron and of Zacharias, accept also from the hand of us sinners this incense for an odour of a sweet smell, and for remission of our sins, and those of all Thy people; for blessed art Thou, and glory becomes Thee, the Father, and the Son, and the Holy Spirit, now and ever.

The Deacon.

Sir, pronounce the blessing.[1]

The Priest prays.

Our Lord and God, Jesus Christ, who through exceeding goodness and love not to be restrained wast crucified, and didst not refuse to be pierced by the spear and nails; who didst provide this mysterious and awful service as an everlasting memorial for us perpetually: bless Thy ministry in Christ the God, and bless our entrance, and fully complete the presentation of this our service by Thy unutterable compassion, now and ever, and to all eternity. Amen.

The responsive prayer from the Deacon.

VI. The Lord bless us, and make us worthy seraphically to offer gifts, and to sing the oft-sung hymn of the divine Trisagion, by the fulness and exceeding abundance of all the perfection of holiness, now and ever.

Then the Deacon begins to sing in the entrance.

Thou who art the only-begotten Son and Word of God, immortal; who didst submit for our salvation to become flesh of the holy God-mother, and ever-virgin Mary; who didst immutably become man and wast crucified, O Christ our God, and didst by Thy death tread death under foot; who art one of the Holy Trinity, glorified together with the Father and the Holy Spirit, save us.

[1] This is addressed to the priest. Some translate, "O Lord, bless us."

The Priest says this prayer from the gates to the altar.

VII. God Almighty, Lord great in glory, who hast given to us an entrance into the Holy of Holies, through the sojourning among men of Thy only-begotten Son, our Lord, and God, and Saviour Jesus Christ, we supplicate and invoke Thy goodness, since we are fearful and trembling when about to stand at Thy holy altar; send forth upon us, O God, Thy good grace, and sanctify our souls, and bodies, and spirits, and turn our thoughts to piety, in order that with a pure conscience we may bring unto Thee gifts, offerings, and fruits for the remission of our transgressions, and for the propitiation of all Thy people, by the grace and mercies and loving-kindness of Thy only-begotten Son, with whom Thou art blessed to all eternity. Amen.

After the approach to the altar, the Priest says:

VIII. Peace be to all.

The People.

And to thy spirit.

The Priest.

The Lord bless us all, and sanctify us for the entrance and celebration of the divine and pure mysteries, giving rest to the blessed souls among the good and just, by His grace and loving-kindness, now and ever, and to all eternity. Amen.

Then the Deacon says the bidding prayer.

IX. In peace let us beseech the Lord.

For the peace that is from above, and for God's love to man, and for the salvation of our souls, let us beseech the Lord.

For the peace of the whole world, for the unity of all the holy churches of God, let us beseech the Lord.

For the remission of our sins, and forgiveness of our transgressions, and for our deliverance from all tribulation, wrath, danger, and distress, and from the uprising of our enemies, let us beseech the Lord.

Then the Singers sing the Trisagion Hymn.

Holy God, holy mighty, holy immortal, have mercy upon us.

Then the Priest prays, bowing.

X. O compassionate and merciful, long-suffering, and very gracious and true God, look from Thy prepared dwelling-place, and hear us Thy suppliants, and deliver us from every temptation of the devil and of man; withhold not Thy aid from us, nor bring on us chastisements too heavy for our strength: for we are unable to overcome what is opposed to us; but Thou art able, Lord, to save us from everything that is against us. Save us, O God, from the difficulties of this world, according to Thy goodness, in order that, having drawn nigh with a pure conscience to Thy holy altar, we may send up to Thee without condemnation the blessed hymn Trisagion, together with the heavenly powers, and that, having performed the service, well pleasing to Thee and divine, we may be counted worthy of eternal life.

Aloud.

Because Thou art holy, Lord our God, and dwellest and abidest in holy places, we send up the praise and the hymn Trisagion to Thee, the Father, and the Son, and the Holy Spirit, now and ever, and to all eternity.

The People.

Amen.

The Priest.

XI. Peace be to all.

The People.

And to thy spirit.

The Singers.

Alleluia.

Then there are read in order the holy oracles of the Old Testament, and of the prophets; and the incarnation of the Son of God is set forth, and His sufferings and resurrection from the dead, His ascension into heaven, and His second appearing with glory; and this takes place daily in the holy and divine service.

After the reading and instruction the Deacon says:

XII. Let us all say, Lord, be merciful.

Lord Almighty, the God of our fathers, we beseech Thee, hear us.

For the peace which is from above, and for the salvation of our souls, let us beseech the Lord.

For the peace of the whole world, and the unity of all the holy churches of God, let us beseech the Lord.

For the salvation and help of all the Christ-loving people, we beseech Thee, hear us.

For our deliverance from all tribulation, wrath, danger, distress, from captivity, bitter death, and from our iniquities, we beseech Thee, hear us.

For the people standing round, and waiting for the rich and plenteous mercy that is from Thee, we beseech Thee, be merciful and gracious.

Save Thy people, O Lord, and bless Thine inheritance.

Visit Thy world in mercy and compassion.

Exalt the horn of Christians by the power of the precious and quickening cross.

We beseech Thee, most merciful Lord, hear us praying to Thee, and have mercy upon us.

The People thrice.

Lord, have mercy upon us.

The Deacon.

XIII. For the remission of our sins, and forgiveness of our transgressions, and for our deliverance from all tribulation, wrath, danger, and distress, let us beseech the Lord.

Let us all entreat from the Lord, that we may pass the whole day, perfect, holy, peaceful, and without sin.

Let us entreat from the Lord a messenger of peace, a faithful guide, a guardian of our souls and bodies.

Let us entreat from the Lord forgiveness and remission of our sins and transgressions.

Let us entreat from the Lord the things which are good and proper for our souls, and peace for the world.

Let us entreat from the Lord, that we may spend the remaining period of our life in peace and health.

Let us entreat that the close of our lives may be Christian, without pain and without shame, and a good plea at the dread and awful judgment-seat of Christ.

The Priest.

XIV. For Thou art the gospel and the light, Saviour and keeper of our souls and bodies, God, and Thy only-begotten Son, and Thy all-holy Spirit, now and ever.

The People.

Amen.

The Priest.

[Commemorating with all the holy and just, our all-holy, pure, most glorious Lady, the God-mother, and ever-virgin Mary, let us devote ourselves, and one another, and our whole life, to Christ our God.]

The People.

To Thee, Lord.

The Priest.

God, who hast taught us Thy divine and saving oracles, enlighten the souls of us sinners for the comprehension of the things which have been before spoken, so that we may not only be seen to be hearers of spiritual things, but also doers of good deeds, striving after guileless faith, blameless life, and pure conversation.

Aloud.

In Christ Jesus our Lord, with whom Thou art blessed,

together with Thy all-holy, good, and quickening Spirit, now and always, and for ever.

The People.

Amen.

The Priest.

XV. Peace be to all.

The People.

And to thy spirit.

The Deacon.

Let us bow our heads to the Lord

The People.

To Thee, Lord.

The Priest prays, saying:

O Sovereign giver of life, and provider of good things, who didst give to mankind the blessed hope of eternal life, our Lord Jesus Christ, count us worthy in holiness, and perfect this Thy divine service to the enjoyment of future blessedness.

Aloud.

So that, guarded by Thy power at all times, and led into the light of truth, we may send up the praise and the thanksgiving to Thee, the Father, the Son, and the Holy Spirit, now and ever.

The People.

Amen.

The Deacon.

XVI. Let none of the catechumens, none of the unbaptized, none of those who are unable to join with us in prayer; look at one another: the door: all erect:[1] let us again pray to the Lord.

---

[1] These clauses are elliptical. After "prayer" supply "remain;" the door is for "shut the door;" and "all erect," for "stand all erect."

The Priest says the prayer of incense.

Sovereign Almighty, King of Glory, who knowest all things before their creation, manifest Thyself to us calling upon Thee at this holy hour, and redeem us from the shame of our transgressions; cleanse our mind and our thoughts from impure desires, from worldly deceit, from all influence of the devil; and accept from the hands of us sinners this incense, as Thou didst accept the offering of Abel, and Noah, and Aaron, and Samuel, and of all Thy saints, guarding us from everything evil, and preserving us for continually pleasing, and worshipping, and glorifying Thee, the Father, and Thy only-begotten Son, and Thy all-holy Spirit, now and always, and for ever.

And the Readers begin the Cherubic Hymn.

Let all mortal flesh be silent, and stand with fear and trembling, and meditate nothing earthly within itself: for the King of kings and Lord of lords, Christ our God, comes forward to be sacrificed, and to be given for food to the faithful; and the bands of angels go before Him with every power and dominion, the many-eyed cherubim, and the six-winged seraphim, covering their faces, and crying aloud the hymn, Alleluia, Alleluia, Alleluia.

The Priest, bringing in the holy gifts, says this prayer:

XVII. O God, our God, who didst send forth the heavenly bread, the food of the whole world, our Lord Jesus Christ, to be a Saviour, and Redeemer, and Benefactor, blessing and sanctifying us, do Thou Thyself bless this offering, and graciously receive it to Thy altar above the skies; remember in Thy goodness and love those who have brought it, and those for whom they have brought it, and preserve us without condemnation in the service of Thy divine mysteries: for hallowed and glorified is Thy all-honoured and great name, Father, and Son, and Holy Spirit, now and ever, and to all eternity.

The Priest.

Peace be to all.

The Deacon.

Sir, pronounce the blessing.

The Priest.

Blessed be God, who blesseth and sanctifieth us all at the presentation of the divine and pure mysteries, and giveth rest to the blessed souls among the holy and just, now and always, and to all eternity.

The Deacon.

XVIII. Let us attend in wisdom.

The Priest begins.

I believe in one God, Father Almighty, Maker of heaven and earth, and in one Lord Jesus Christ, the Son of God. *And the rest of the creed.*

Then he prays, bowing his neck.

XIX. God and Sovereign of all, make us, who are unworthy, worthy of this hour, lover of mankind; that being pure from all deceit and all hypocrisy, we may be united with one another by the bond of peace and love, being confirmed by the sanctification of Thy divine knowledge through Thine only-begotten Son, our Lord and Saviour Jesus Christ, with whom Thou art blessed, together with Thy all-holy, and good, and quickening Spirit, now and ever, and to all eternity. Amen.

The Deacon.

XX. Let us stand well, let us stand reverently, let us stand in the fear of God, and with compunction of heart. In peace let us pray to the Lord.

The Priest.

For God of peace, mercy, love, compassion, and loving-kindness art Thou, and Thine only-begotten Son, and Thine all-holy Spirit, now and ever.

The People.

Amen.

The Priest.

Peace be to all.

The People.

And to thy spirit.

The Deacon.

Let us salute one another with an holy kiss. Let us bow our heads to the Lord.

The Priest bows, saying this prayer:

XXI. Only Lord and merciful God, on those who are bowing their necks before Thy holy altar, and seeking the spiritual gifts that come from Thee, send forth Thy good grace; and bless us all with every spiritual blessing, that cannot be taken from us, Thou, who dwellest on high, and hast regard unto things that are lowly.

Aloud.

For worthy of praise and worship and most glorious is Thy all-holy name, Father and Son and Holy Spirit, now and always, and to all eternity.

The Deacon.

Sir, pronounce the blessing.

The Priest.

The Lord will bless us, and minister with us all by His grace and loving-kindness.

And again.

The Lord will bless us, and make us worthy to stand at His holy altar, at all times, now and always, and for ever.

And again.

Blessed be God, who blesseth and sanctifieth us all in our

attendance upon, and service of, His pure mysteries, now and always, and for ever.

The Deacon makes the Universal Collect.

XXII. In peace let us pray to the Lord.

The People.

O Lord, have mercy.

The Deacon.

Save us, have mercy upon us, pity and keep us, O God, by Thy grace.

For the peace that is from above, and the loving-kindness of God, and the salvation of our souls, let us beseech the Lord.

For the peace of the whole world, and the unity of all the holy churches of God, let us beseech the Lord.

For those who bear fruit, and labour honourably in the holy churches of God; for those who remember the poor, the widows and the orphans, the strangers and needy ones; and for those who have requested us to mention them in our prayers, let us beseech the Lord.

For those who are in old age and infirmity, for the sick and suffering, and those who are troubled by unclean spirits, for their speedy cure from God and their salvation, let us beseech the Lord.

For those who are passing their days in virginity, and celibacy, and discipline, and for those in holy matrimony; and for the holy fathers and brethren agonizing in mountains, and dens, and caves of the earth, let us beseech the Lord.

For Christians sailing, travelling, living among strangers, and for our brethren in captivity, in exile, in prison, and in bitter slavery, their peaceful return, let us beseech the Lord.

For the remission of our sins, and forgiveness of our transgressions, and for our deliverance from all tribulation, wrath, danger, and constraint, and uprising against us of enemies, let us beseech the Lord.

For favourable weather, peaceful showers, beneficent dews,

abundance of fruits, the perfect close of a good season, and for the crown of the year, let us beseech the Lord.

For our fathers and brethren present, and praying with us in this holy hour, and at every season, their zeal, labour, and earnestness, let us beseech the Lord.

For every Christian soul in tribulation and distress, and needing the mercy and succour of God; for the return of the erring, the health of the sick, the deliverance of the captives, the rest of the fathers and brethren that have fallen asleep aforetime, let us beseech the Lord.

For the hearing and acceptance of our prayer before God, and the sending down on us His rich mercies and compassion, let us beseech the Lord.

Let us commemorate our all-holy, pure, most glorious, blessed lady, God-mother, and ever virgin Mary, and all the holy and just, that we may all find mercy through their prayers and intercessions.

And for the offered, precious, heavenly, unutterable, pure, glorious, dread, awful, divine gifts, and the salvation of the priest who stands by and offers them, let us offer supplication to God the Lord.

The People.

O Lord, have mercy.

Thrice.

Then the Priest makes the sign of the cross on the gifts, and standing, speaks separately thus:

XXIII. Glory to God in the highest, and on earth peace, goodwill among men.

Thrice.

Lord, Thou wilt open my lips, and my mouth shall show forth Thy praise.

Thrice.

Let my mouth be filled with Thy praise, O Lord, that I may tell of Thy glory, of Thy majesty, all the day.

Thrice.

Of the Father. Amen. And of the Son. Amen. And of the Holy Spirit. Amen. Now and always, and to all eternity. Amen.

And bowing to this side and to that, he says:

XXIV. Magnify the Lord with me, and let us exalt His name together.

And they answer, bowing:

The Holy Ghost shall come upon thee, and the power of the Highest shall overshadow thee.

Then the Priest, at great length:

O Sovereign Lord, who hast visited us in compassion and mercies, and hast freely given to us, Thy humble and sinful and unworthy servants, boldness to stand at Thy holy altar, and to offer to Thee this dread and bloodless sacrifice for our sins, and for the errors of the people, look upon me Thy unprofitable servant, and blot out my transgressions for Thy compassion's sake; and purify my lips and heart from all pollution of flesh and spirit; and remove from me every shameful and foolish thought, and fit me by the power of Thy all-holy Spirit for this service; and receive me graciously by Thy goodness as I draw nigh to Thy altar; and be pleased, O Lord, that these gifts brought by our hands may be acceptable, stooping to my weakness; and cast me not away from Thy presence, and abhor not my unworthiness; but pity me according to Thy great mercy, and according to the multitude of Thy mercies pass by my transgressions, that, having come before Thy glory without condemnation, I may be counted worthy of the protection of Thy only-begotten Son, and of the illumination of Thy all-holy Spirit, that I may not be as a slave of sin cast out, but as Thy servant may find grace and mercy and forgiveness of sins before Thee, both in the world that now is and in that which is to come. I beseech Thee, Almighty Sovereign, all-powerful

Lord, hear my prayer; for Thou art He who workest all in all, and we all seek in all things the help and succour that come from Thee and Thy only-begotten Son, and the good and quickening and consubstantial Spirit, now and ever.

XXV. O God, who through Thy great and unspeakable love didst send forth Thy only-begotten Son into the world, in order that He might turn back the lost sheep, turn not away us sinners, laying hold of Thee by this dread and bloodless sacrifice; for we trust not in our own righteousness, but in Thy good mercy, by which Thou purchasest our race. We entreat and beseech Thy goodness that it may not be for condemnation to Thy people that this mystery for salvation has been administered by us, but for remission of sins, for renewal of souls and bodies, for the well-pleasing of Thee, God and Father, in the mercy and love of Thy only-begotten Son, with whom Thou art blessed, together with Thy all-holy and good and quickening Spirit, now and always, and for ever.

XXVI. O Lord God, who didst create us, and bring us into life, who hast shown to us ways to salvation, who hast granted to us a revelation of heavenly mysteries, and hast appointed us to this ministry in the power of Thy all-holy Spirit, grant, O Sovereign, that we may become servants of Thy new testament, ministers of Thy pure mysteries, and receive us as we draw near to Thy holy altar, according to the greatness of Thy mercy, that we may become worthy of offering to Thee gifts and sacrifices for our transgressions and for those of the people; and grant to us, O Lord, with all fear and a pure conscience to offer to Thee this spiritual and bloodless sacrifice, and graciously receiving it unto Thy holy and spiritual altar above the skies for an odour of a sweet spiritual smell, send down in answer on us the grace of Thy all-holy Spirit. And, O God, look upon us, and have regard to this our reasonable service, and accept it, as Thou didst accept the gifts of Abel, the sacrifices of Noah, the priestly offices of Moses and Aaron, the peace-offerings of Samuel, the repentance of David, the incense of Zacharias. As Thou didst accept from the hand of Thy apostles this true service, so accept also in Thy goodness from the hands of us sinners these offered gifts;

and grant that our offering may be acceptable, sanctified by the Holy Spirit, as a propitiation for our transgressions and the errors of the people, and for the rest of the souls that have fallen asleep aforetime; that we also, Thy humble, sinful, and unworthy servants, being counted worthy without guile to serve Thy holy altar, may receive the reward of faithful and wise stewards, and may find grace and mercy in the terrible day of Thy just and good retribution.

Prayer of the veil.

XXVII. We thank Thee, O Lord our God, that Thou hast given us boldness for the entrance of Thy holy places, which Thou hast renewed to us as a new and living way through the veil of the flesh of Thy Christ. We therefore, being counted worthy to enter into the place of the tabernacle of Thy glory, and to be within the veil, and to behold the Holy of Holies, cast ourselves down before Thy goodness: Lord, have mercy on us: since we are full of fear and trembling, when about to stand at Thy holy altar, and to offer this dread and bloodless sacrifice for our own sins and for the errors of the people: send forth, O God, Thy good grace, and sanctify our souls, and bodies, and spirits; and turn our thoughts to holiness, that with a pure conscience we may bring to Thee an offering of peace, a sacrifice of praise.

Aloud.

By the mercy and loving-kindness of Thy only-begotten Son, with whom Thou art blessed, together with Thy all-holy, and good, and quickening Spirit, now and always.

The People.

Amen.

The Priest.

Peace be to all.

The Deacon.

Let us stand reverently, let us stand in the fear of God, and with contrition: let us attend to the holy communion service, to offer peace to God.

The People.

An offering of peace, a sacrifice of praise,

The Priest.

And, uncovering the robes that darkly invest in symbol this sacred ceremonial, do Thou reveal it clearly to us: fill our intellectual vision with absolute light, and having purified our poverty from every pollution of flesh and spirit, make it worthy of this dread and awful approach: for Thou art an all-merciful and gracious God, and we send up the praise and the thanksgiving to Thee, Father, Son, and Holy Spirit, now, and always, and for ever.

Then he says aloud:

XXVIII. The love of the Lord and Father, the grace of the Lord and Son, and the fellowship and the gift of the Holy Spirit, be with us all.

The People.

And with thy spirit.

The Priest.

Let us lift up our minds and our hearts.

The People.

It is becoming and right.

Then the Priest prays.

Verily it is becoming and right, proper and due to praise Thee, to sing of Thee, to bless Thee, to worship Thee, to glorify Thee, to give Thee thanks, Maker of every creature visible and invisible, the treasure of eternal good things, the fountain of life and immortality, God and Lord of all, whom the heavens of heavens praise, and all the host of them; the sun, and the moon, and all the choir of the stars; earth, sea, and all that is in them; Jerusalem, the heavenly assembly, and church of the first-born that are written in heaven; spirits of just men and of prophets; souls of martyrs and of apostles;

angels, archangels, thrones, dominions, principalities, and authorities, and dread powers; and the many-eyed cherubim, and the six-winged seraphim, which cover their faces with two wings, their feet with two, and with two they fly, crying one to another with unresting lips, with unceasing praises.

Aloud.

With loud voice singing the victorious hymn of Thy majestic glory, crying aloud, praising, shouting, and saying;

The People.

Holy, holy, holy, O Lord of Sabaoth, the heaven and the earth are full of Thy glory. Hosanna in the highest; blessed is He that cometh in the name of the Lord. Hosanna in the highest.

The Priest, making the sign of the cross on the gifts, says:

XXIX. Holy art Thou, King of eternity, and Lord and giver of all holiness; holy also Thy only-begotten Son, our Lord Jesus Christ, by whom Thou hast made all things; holy also Thy Holy Spirit, which searches all things, even Thy deep things, O God: holy art Thou, almighty, all-powerful, good, dread, merciful, most compassionate to Thy creatures; who didst make man from earth after Thine own image and likeness; who didst give him the joy of paradise; and when he transgressed Thy commandment, and fell away, didst not disregard nor desert him, O Good One, but didst chasten him as a merciful father, call him by the law, instruct him by the prophets; and afterwards didst send forth Thine only-begotten Son Himself, our Lord Jesus Christ, into the world, that He by His coming might renew and restore Thy image; who, having descended from heaven, and become flesh of the Holy Spirit and Virgin God-mother Mary, and having sojourned among men, fulfilled the dispensation for the salvation of our race; and being about to endure His voluntary and life-giving death by the cross, He the sinless for us the sinners, in the night in which He was betrayed, nay, rather delivered Himself up for the life and salvation of the world,

Then the Priest holds the bread in his hand, and says:

XXX. Having taken the bread in His holy and pure and blameless and immortal hands, lifting up His eyes to heaven, and showing it to Thee, His God and Father, He gave thanks, and hallowed, and broke, and gave it to us, His disciples and apostles, saying:

The Deacons say:

For the remission of sins and life everlasting.

Then he says aloud:

Take, eat: this is my body, broken for you, and given for remission of sins.

The People.

Amen.

Then he takes the cup, and says:

In like manner, after supper, He took the cup, and having mixed wine and water, lifting up His eyes to heaven, and presenting it to Thee, His God and Father, He gave thanks, and hallowed and blessed it, and filled it with the Holy Spirit, and gave it to us His disciples, saying, Drink ye all of it; this is my blood of the new testament shed for you and many, and distributed for the remission of sins.

The People.

Amen.

The Priest.

This do in remembrance of me; for as often as ye eat this bread, and drink this cup, ye do show forth the Lord's death, and confess His resurrection, till He come.

The Deacons say:

We believe and confess.

The People.

We show forth Thy death, O Lord, and confess Thy resurrection.

The Priest.

XXXI. Remembering, therefore, His life-giving sufferings, His saving cross, His death and His burial, and resurrection from the dead on the third day, and His ascension into heaven, and sitting at the right hand of Thee, our God and Father, and His second glorious and awful appearing, when He shall come with glory to judge the quick and the dead, and render to every one according to His works; even we, sinful men, offer unto Thee, O Lord, this dread and bloodless sacrifice, praying that Thou wilt not deal with us after our sins, nor reward us according to our iniquities; but that Thou, according to Thy mercy and Thy unspeakable lovingkindness, passing by and blotting out the handwriting against us Thy suppliants, wilt grant to us Thy heavenly and eternal gifts, which eye hath not seen, and ear hath not heard, and which have not entered into the heart of man (to conceive) that Thou hast prepared, O God, for those who love Thee; and reject not, O loving Lord, the people for my sake, or for my sin's sake.

Then he says, thrice:

For Thy people and Thy church supplicate Thee.

The People.

Have mercy on us, O Lord our God, Father Almighty.

Again the Priest says:

XXXII. Have mercy upon us, O God Almighty.
Have mercy upon us, O God our Saviour.
Have mercy upon us, O God, according to Thy great mercy, and send forth on us, and on these offered gifts, Thy all-holy Spirit.

Then, bowing his neck, he says:

The sovereign and quickening Spirit, that sits upon the throne with Thee, our God and Father, and with Thy only-begotten Son, reigning with Thee; the consubstantial and co-eternal; that spoke in the law and in the prophets, and in Thy New Testament; that descended in the form of a dove on our Lord Jesus Christ at the river Jordan, and abode on Him; that descended on Thy apostles in the form of tongues of fire in the upper room of the holy and glorious Zion on the day of Pentecost: this Thine all-holy Spirit, send down, O Lord, upon us, and upon these offered holy gifts;

And rising up, he says aloud:

That coming, by His holy and good and glorious appearing, He may sanctify this bread, and make it the holy body of Thy Christ.

The People.

Amen.

The Priest.

And this cup the precious blood of Thy Christ.

The People.

Amen.

The Priest by himself standing.

XXXIII. That they may be to all that partake of them for remission of sins, and for life everlasting, for the sanctification of souls and of bodies, for bearing the fruit of good works, for the stablishing of Thy holy catholic church, which Thou hast founded on the rock of faith, that the gates of hell may not prevail against it; delivering it from all heresy and scandals, and from those who work iniquity, keeping it till the fulness of the time.

And having bowed, he says:

XXXIV. We present them to Thee also, O Lord, for the holy places, which Thou hast glorified by the divine appearing of Thy Christ, and by the visitation of Thy all-holy Spirit; especially for the glorious Zion, the mother of all the churches; and for Thy holy, catholic, and apostolic church throughout the world: even now, O Lord, bestow upon her the rich gifts of Thy all-holy Spirit.

Remember also, O Lord, our holy fathers and brethren in it, and the bishops in all the world, who rightly divide the word of Thy truth.

Remember also, O Lord, every city and country, and those of the true faith dwelling in them, their peace and security.

Remember, O Lord, Christians sailing, travelling, sojourning in strange lands; our fathers and brethren, who are in bonds, prison, captivity, and exile; who are in mines, and under torture, and in bitter slavery.

Remember, O Lord, the sick and afflicted, and those troubled by unclean spirits, their speedy healing from Thee, O God, and their salvation.

Remember, O Lord, every Christian soul in affliction and distress, needing Thy mercy and succour, O God; and the return of the erring.

Remember, O Lord, our fathers and brethren, toiling hard, and ministering unto us, for Thy holy name's sake.

Remember all, O Lord, for good: have mercy on all, O Lord, be reconciled to us all: give peace to the multitudes of Thy people: put away scandals: bring wars to an end: make the uprising of heresies to cease: grant Thy peace and Thy love to us, O God our Saviour, the hope of all the ends of the earth.

Remember, O Lord, favourable weather, peaceful showers, beneficent dews, abundance of fruits, and to crown the year with Thy goodness; for the eyes of all wait on Thee, and Thou givest their food in due season: thou openest Thy hand, and fillest every living thing with gladness.

Remember, O Lord, those who bear fruit, and labour honourably in the holy (services) of Thy church; and those who forget not the poor, the widows, the orphans, the strangers, and the needy; and all who have desired us to remember them in our prayers. Moreover, O Lord, be pleased to remember those who have brought these offerings this day to Thy holy altar, and for what each one has brought them or with what mind, and those persons who have just now been mentioned to Thee.

Remember, O Lord, according to the multitude of Thy mercy and compassion, me also, Thy humble and unprofitable servant; and the deacons who surround Thy holy altar, and graciously give them a blameless life, keep their ministry undefiled, and purchase for them a good degree, that we may find mercy and grace, with all the saints that have been well pleasing to Thee since the world began, to generation and generation—grandsires, sires, patriarchs, prophets, apostles, martyrs, confessors, teachers, saints, and every just spirit made perfect in the faith of Thy Christ.

XXXV. Hail, Mary, highly favoured: the Lord is with Thee; blessed art thou among women, and blessed the fruit of thy womb, for thou didst bear the Saviour of our souls.

Then the Priest says aloud:

Hail in the highest, our all-holy, pure, most blessed, glorious Lady, the God-mother and ever-virgin Mary.

The Singers.

Verily it is becoming to bless Thee, the God-bearing, the ever-blessed, and all-blameless, and mother of our God; more honourable than the cherubim, and incomparably more glorious than the seraphim: thee, who didst bear with purity God the Word, thee the true God-mother, we magnify.

And again they sing:

In thee, highly favoured, all creation rejoices, the host of angels, and the race of men; hallowed temple, and spiritual paradise, pride of virgins, of whom God was made flesh and our God, who was before eternity, became a little child: for He made Thy womb His throne, and Thy belly broader than the heavens. In thee, O highly favoured one, all creation rejoices: glory unto thee.

The Deacons.

XXXVI. Remember us, O Lord God.

The Priest, bowing, says:

Remember, O Lord God, the spirits and all flesh, of whom we have made mention, and of whom we have not made mention, who are of the true faith, from righteous Abel unto this day: unto them do Thou give rest there in the land of the living, in Thy kingdom, in the joy of paradise, in the bosom of Abraham, and of Isaac, and of Jacob, our holy fathers; whence pain, and grief, and lamentation have fled: there the light of Thy countenance looks upon them, and enlightens them for ever. Make the end of our lives Christian, acceptable, blameless, and peaceful, O Lord, O Lord, gathering us together under the feet of Thine elect, when Thou wilt, and as Thou wilt; only without shame and transgressions, through Thy only-begotten Son, our Lord and God and Saviour Jesus Christ: for He is the only sinless one who hath appeared on the earth.

The Deacon.

And for the peace and stablishing of the whole world, and of the holy churches of God, and for the purposes for which each one made his offering, or according to the desire he has: and for the people standing round, and for all men, and all women.

The People.

And for all men and all women.

The Priest says aloud:

Wherefore, both to them and to us, do Thou in Thy goodness and love,

The People.

Forgive, remit, pardon, O God, our transgressions, voluntary and involuntary: in deed and in word: in knowledge and in ignorance: by night and by day: in thought and intent: in Thy goodness and love, forgive us them all.

The Priest.

Through the grace and compassion and love of Thy only-begotten Son, with whom Thou art blessed and glorified, together with the all-holy, and good, and quickening Spirit, now and ever, and to all eternity.

The People.

Amen.

The Priest.

XXXVII. Peace be to all.

The People.

And to thy spirit.

The Deacon.

Again, and continually, in peace let us pray to the Lord. For the gifts to the Lord God presented and sanctified, precious, heavenly, unspeakable, pure, glorious, dread, awful, divine, let us pray.

That the Lord our God, having graciously received them to His altar that is holy and above the heavens, rational and spiritual, for the odour of a sweet spiritual savour, may send down in answer upon us the divine grace and the gift of the all-holy Spirit, let us pray.

Having prayed for the unity of the faith, and the communion of His all-holy and adorable Spirit, let us commend ourselves and one another, and our whole life, to Christ our God.

The People.

Amen.

The Priest prays.

XXXVIII. God and Father of our Lord and God and Saviour Jesus Christ, the glorious Lord, the blessed essence, the bounteous goodness, the God and Sovereign of all, who art blessed to all eternity, who sittest upon the cherubim, and art glorified by the seraphim, before whom stand thousand thousands and ten thousand times ten thousand hosts of angels and archangels: Thou hast accepted the gifts, offerings, and fruits brought unto Thee as an odour of a sweet spiritual smell, and hast been pleased to sanctify them, and make them perfect, O good One, by the grace of Thy Christ, and by the presence of Thy all-holy Spirit. Sanctify also, O Lord, our souls, and bodies, and spirits, and touch our understandings, and search our consciences, and cast out from us every evil imagination, every impure feeling, every base desire, every unbecoming thought, all envy, and vanity, and hypocrisy, all lying, all deceit, every worldly affection, all covetousness, all vainglory, all indifference, all vice, all passion, all anger, all malice, all blasphemy, every motion of the flesh and spirit that is not in accordance with Thy holy will.

Aloud.

And count us worthy, O loving Lord, with boldness, without condemnation, in a pure heart, with a contrite spirit, with unshamed face, with sanctified lips, to dare to call upon Thee, the holy God, Father in heaven, and to say,

The People.

Our Father, which art in heaven : hallowed be Thy name ; *and so on.*

The Priest, bowing, says :

And lead us not into temptation, Lord, Lord of Hosts, who knowest our frailty, but deliver us from the evil one and his works, and from all his malice and craftiness, for the sake of Thy holy name, which has been placed upon our humility.

Aloud.

For Thine is the kingdom, the power, and the glory, Father, Son, and Holy Spirit, now and for ever.

The People.

Amen.

The Priest.

XXXIX. Peace be to all.

The People.

And to thy spirit.

The Deacon.

Let us bow our heads to the Lord.

The People.

To Thee, O Lord.

The Priest prays, speaking thus:

To Thee, O Lord, we Thy servants have bowed our heads before Thy holy altar, waiting for the rich mercies that are from Thee. Send forth upon us, O Lord, Thy plenteous grace and Thy blessing; and sanctify our souls, bodies, and spirits, that we may become worthy communicants and partakers of Thy holy mysteries, to the forgiveness of sins and life everlasting.

Aloud.

For adorable and glorified art Thou, our God, and Thy only-begotten Son, and Thy all-holy Spirit, now and ever.

The People.

Amen.

The Priest says aloud:

And the grace and the mercies of the holy and consubstantial, and uncreated, and adorable Trinity, shall be with us all.

The People.

And with thy spirit.

The Deacon.

In the fear of God, let us attend.

The Priest, elevating the gifts, says secretly:

O holy Lord, that abidest in holy places, sanctify us by the word of Thy grace, and by the visitation of Thy all-holy

Spirit: for Thou, O Lord, hast said, Ye will be holy, for I am holy. O Lord our God, incomprehensible Word of God, one in substance with the Father and the Holy Spirit, co-eternal and indivisible, accept the pure hymn, in Thy holy and bloodless sacrifices; with the cherubim, and seraphim, and from me, a sinful man, crying and saying,

Aloud.

XL. The holy things unto the holy.

The People.

One holy, one Lord Jesus Christ, to the glory of God the Father, to whom be glory to all eternity.

The Deacon.

XLI. For the remission of our sins, and the propitiation of our souls, and for every soul in tribulation and distress, needing the mercy and succour of God, and for the return of the erring, the healing of the sick, the deliverance of the captives, the rest of our fathers and brethren, who have fallen asleep aforetime, let us all say fervently, Lord, have mercy.

The People.

Lord, have mercy. *Twelve times.*

Then the Priest breaks the bread, and holds the half in his right hand, and the half in his left, and dips that in his right hand in the chalice, saying:

The union of the all-holy body and precious blood of our Lord and God and Saviour, Jesus Christ.

Then he makes the sign of the cross on that in his left hand: then with that which has been signed the other half: then forthwith he begins to divide, and before all to give to each chalice a single piece, saying:

It has been made one, and sanctified, and perfected, in the name of the Father, and of the Son, and of the Holy Spirit, now and ever.

And when he makes the sign of the cross on the bread, he says:

Behold the Lamb of God, the Son of the Father, that taketh away the sin of the world, sacrificed for the life and salvation of the world.

And when he gives a single piece to each chalice, he says:

A holy portion of Christ, full of grace and truth, of the Father, and of the Holy Spirit, to whom be the glory and the power to all eternity.

Then he begins to divide, and to say:

XLII. The Lord is my Shepherd, I shall not want. In green pastures, *and so on* (Ps. xxiii.).

Then,

I will bless the Lord at all times, *and so on* (Ps. xxxiv.).

Then,

I will extol Thee, my God, O King, *and so on* (Ps. cxlv.).

Then,

O praise the Lord, all ye nations, *and so on* (Ps. cxvii.).

The Deacon.

Sir, pronounce the blessing.

The Priest.

The Lord will bless us, and keep us without condemnation for the participation of His pure gifts, now and always, and for ever.

And when they have filled, the Deacon says:

Sir, pronounce the blessing.

The Priest says:

The Lord will bless us, and make us worthy with the pure touchings of our fingers to take the live coal, and place it upon the mouths of the faithful for the purification and renewal of their souls and bodies, now and always.

Then,

O taste and see that the Lord is good, who is parted and not divided, distributed to the faithful and not expended, for the remission of sins, and the life everlasting, now and always, and for ever.

The Deacon.

In the peace of Christ, let us sing.

The Singers.

O taste and see that the Lord is good.

The Priest says the prayer before the communion.

O Lord our God, the heavenly bread, the life of the universe, I have sinned against Heaven, and before Thee, and am not worthy to partake of Thy pure mysteries; but as a merciful God, make me worthy by Thy grace, without condemnation to partake of Thy holy body and precious blood, for the remission of sins, and life everlasting.

XLIII. *Then he distributes to the clergy; and when the deacons take the disks*[1] *and the chalices for distribution to the people, the Deacon, who takes the first disk, says,*

Sir, pronounce the blessing.

The Priest replies:

Glory to God who has sanctified and is sanctifying us all.

The Deacon says:

Be Thou exalted, O God, over the heavens, and Thy glory over all the earth, and Thy kingdom endureth to all eternity.

And when the Deacon is about to put it on the side-table, the Priest says:

Blessed be the name of the Lord our God for ever.

[1] Or patena.

The Deacon.

In the fear of God, and in faith and love, draw nigh.

The People.

Blessed is He that cometh in the name of the Lord.

And again, when he lifts the disk from the side-table, he says:
Sir, pronounce the blessing.

The Priest.

Save Thy people, O God, and bless Thine inheritance.

The Priest again.

Glory to our God, who has sanctified us all.

And when he has put the chalice back on the holy table, the Priest says:
Blessed be the name of the Lord to all eternity.

The Deacons and the People say:

Fill our mouths with Thy praise, O Lord, and fill our lips with joy, that we may sing of Thy glory, of Thy greatness all the day.

And again:

We render thanks to Thee, Christ our God, that Thou hast made us worthy to partake of Thy body and blood, for the remission of sins, and for life everlasting. Do Thou, in Thy goodness and love, keep us, we pray Thee, without condemnation.

The prayer of incense at the last entrance.

XLIV. We render thanks to Thee, the Saviour and God of all, for all the good things Thou hast given us, and for the participation of Thy holy and pure mysteries, and we offer to Thee this incense, praying: Keep us under the shadow of Thy wings, and count us worthy till our last breath to partake of Thy holy rites for the sanctification of our souls and bodies, for the inheritance of the kingdom of heaven: for Thou, O God, art our sanctification, and we send up praise and thanksgiving to Thee, Father, Son, and Holy Spirit.

The Deacon begins in the entrance.

Glory to Thee, glory to Thee, glory to Thee, O Christ the King, only-begotten Word of the Father, that Thou hast counted us, Thy sinful and unworthy servants, worthy to enjoy thy pure mysteries for the remission of sins, and for life everlasting: glory to Thee.

And when he has made the entrance, the Deacon begins to speak thus:

XLV. Again and again, and at all times, in peace, let us beseech the Lord.

That the participation of His holy rites may be to us for the turning away from every wicked thing, for our support on the journey to life everlasting, for the communion and gift of the Holy Spirit, let us pray.

The Priest prays.

Commemorating our all-holy, pure, most glorious, blessed Lady, the God-Mother and Ever-Virgin Mary, and all the saints that have been well-pleasing to Thee since the world began, let us devote ourselves, and one another, and our whole life, to Christ our God.

The People.

To Thee, O Lord.

The Priest.

XLVI. O God, who through Thy great and unspeakable love didst condescend to the weakness of Thy servants, and hast counted us worthy to partake of this heavenly table, condemn not us sinners for the participation of Thy pure mysteries; but keep us, O good One, in the sanctification of Thy Holy Spirit, that being made holy, we may find part and inheritance with all Thy saints that have been well-pleasing to Thee since the world began, in the light of Thy countenance, through the mercy of Thy only-begotten Son, our Lord and God and Saviour Jesus Christ, with whom Thou art blessed, together with Thy all-holy, and good, and quickening Spirit: for blessed and glorified is Thy all-precious and glorious name, Father, Son, and Holy Spirit, now and ever, and to all eternity.

The People.

Amen.

The Priest.

Peace be to all.

The People.

And to thy spirit.

The Deacon.

XLVII. Let us bow our heads to the Lord.

The Priest.

O God, great and marvellous, look upon Thy servants, for we have bowed our heads to Thee. Stretch forth Thy hand, strong and full of blessings, and bless Thy people. Keep Thine inheritance, that always and at all times we may glorify Thee, our only living and true God, the holy and consubstantial Trinity, Father, Son, and Holy Ghost, now and ever, and to all eternity.

Aloud.

For unto Thee is becoming and is due praise from us all, and honour, and adoration, and thanksgiving, Father, Son, and Holy Spirit, now and ever.

The Deacon.

XLVIII. In the peace of Christ let us sing.

And again he says:

In the peace of Christ let us go on.

The People.

In the name of the Lord. Sir, pronounce the blessing.

Dismission prayer, spoken by the Deacon.

Going on from glory to glory, we praise Thee, the Saviour of our souls. Glory to Father, and Son, and Holy Spirit now and ever, and to all eternity. We praise Thee, the Saviour of our souls.

The Priest says a prayer from the altar to the sacristy.

XLIX. Going on from strength to strength, and having fulfilled all the divine service in Thy temple, even now we beseech Thee, O Lord our God, make us worthy of perfect loving-kindness; make straight our path: root us in Thy fear, and make us worthy of the heavenly kingdom, in Christ Jesus our Lord, with whom Thou art blessed, together with Thy all-holy, and good, and quickening Spirit, now and always, and for ever.

The Deacon.

L. Again and again, and at all times, in peace let us beseech the Lord.

Prayer said in the sacristy after the dismissal.

Thou hast given unto us, O Lord, sanctification in the communion of the all-holy body and precious blood of Thy only-begotten Son, our Lord Jesus Christ; give unto us also the grace of Thy good Spirit, and keep us blameless in the faith, lead us unto perfect adoption and redemption, and to the coming joys of eternity; for Thou art our sanctification and light, O God, and Thy only-begotten Son, and Thy all-holy Spirit, now and ever, and to all eternity. Amen.

The Deacon.

In the peace of Christ let us keep watch.

The Priest.

Blessed is God, who blesseth and sanctifieth through the communion of the holy, and quickening, and pure mysteries, now and ever, and to all eternity. Amen.

Then the prayer of propitiation.

O Lord Jesus Christ, Son of the living God, Lamb and Shepherd, who takest away the sin of the world, who didst freely forgive their debt to the two debtors, and gavest remission of her sins to the woman that was a sinner, who gavest healing to the paralytic, with the remission of his sins; forgive, remit, pardon, O God, our offences, voluntary and involuntary, in knowledge and in ignorance, by transgression and by disobedience, which Thy all-holy Spirit knows better than Thy servants do: and if men, carnal and dwelling in this world, have in aught erred from Thy commandments, either moved by the devil, whether in word or in deed, or if they have come under a curse, or by reason of some special vow, I entreat and beseech Thy unspeakable lovingkindness, that they may be set free from their word, and released from the oath and the special vow, according to Thy goodness. Verily, O Sovereign Lord, hear my supplication on behalf of Thy servants, and do Thou pass by all their errors, remembering them no more; forgive them every transgression, voluntary and involuntary; deliver them from everlasting punishment: for Thou art He that hast commanded us, saying, Whatsoever things ye bind upon earth, shall be bound in heaven; and whatsoever things ye loose upon earth, shall be loosed in heaven: for thou art our God, a God able to pity, and to save and to forgive sins; and glory is due unto Thee, with the eternal Father, and the quickening Spirit, now and ever, and to all eternity. Amen.

II.
THE DIVINE LITURGY OF THE HOLY APOSTLE AND EVANGELIST MARK,
THE DISCIPLE OF THE HOLY PETER.

The Priest.

I. PEACE be to all.

The People.

And to thy spirit.

The Deacon.

Pray.

The People.

Lord, have mercy; Lord, have mercy; Lord, have mercy.

The Priest prays.

We give Thee thanks, yea, more than thanks, O Lord our God, the Father of our Lord and God and Saviour Jesus Christ, for all Thy goodness at all times and in all places, because Thou hast shielded, rescued, helped, and guided us all the days of our lives, and brought us unto this hour, permitting us again to stand before Thee in Thy holy place, that we may implore forgiveness of our sins and propitiation to all Thy people. We pray and beseech Thee, merciful God, to grant in Thy goodness that we may spend this holy day and all the time of our lives without sin, in fulness of joy, health, safety, holiness, and reverence of Thee. But all envy, all fear, all temptation, all the influence of Satan, all the snares of wicked men, do Thou, O Lord, drive away from us, and from Thy holy catholic and apostolic church. Bestow upon us, O Lord, what is good and meet. Whatever sin we commit in thought, word, or deed, do Thou in Thy goodness and mercy be pleased to pardon. Leave us not, O Lord, while we hope in Thee; nor lead us into temptation, but deliver us from the evil one and from his works, through the grace, mercy, and love of Thine only-begotten Son.

In a loud voice.

Through whom and with whom be glory and power to Thee, in Thy most holy, good, and life-giving Spirit, now, henceforth, and for evermore.

The People.

Amen.

The Priest.

II. Peace be to all.

The People.

And to thy spirit.

The Deacon.

Pray for the king.[1]

The People.

Lord, have mercy; Lord, have mercy; Lord, have mercy.

The Priest prays.

O God, Sovereign Lord, the Father of our Lord and God and Saviour Jesus Christ, we pray and beseech Thee to grant that our king may enjoy peace, and be just and brave. Subdue under him, O God, all his adversaries and enemies. Gird on Thy shield and armour, and rise to his aid. Give him the victory, O God, that his heart may be set on peace

---

[1] Rather "for the emperor," says Renaudot; and the word βασιλεύς will stand this meaning.

and the praise of Thy holy name, that we too in his peaceful reign may spend a calm and tranquil life in all reverence and godly fear, through the grace, mercy, and love of Thine only-begotten Son.

In a loud voice.

Through whom and with whom be glory and power to Thee, with Thy most holy, good, and life-giving Spirit, now, henceforth, and for evermore.

The People.

Amen.

The Priest.

III. Peace be to all.

The People.

And to thy spirit.

The Deacon.

Pray for the pope and the bishop.

The People.

Lord, have mercy; Lord, have mercy; Lord, have mercy.

The Priest.

O Sovereign and Almighty God, the Father of our Lord, God, and Saviour Jesus Christ, we pray and beseech Thee to defend in Thy good mercy our most holy and blessed high priest Pope Δ,[1] and our most reverend Bishop Δ. Preserve them for us through many years in peace, while they according to Thy holy and blessed will fulfil the sacred priesthood committed to their care, and dispense aright the word of truth; with all the orthodox bishops, elders, deacons, sub-deacons, readers, singers, and laity, with the entire body of the holy

[1] The Patriarch of Alexandria is meant. The word πάπας was used at first to designate all bishops; but its application gradually became more restricted, and so here the Patriarch of Alexandria is called πάπας, as being superior to the bishops of his patriarchate.

and only catholic church. Graciously bestow upon them peace, health, and salvation. The prayers they offer up for us, and we for them, do Thou, O Lord, receive at Thy holy, heavenly, and reasonable altar. But all the enemies of Thy holy church put Thou speedily under their feet, through the grace, mercy, and love of Thine only-begotten Son.

Aloud.

Through whom and with whom be glory and power to Thee, with Thy all-holy, good, and life-giving Spirit, now, henceforth, and for evermore.

The People.

Amen.

The Priest.

IV. Peace be to all.

The People.

And to thy spirit.

The Deacon.

Stand and pray.

The People.

Lord have mercy (*thrice*).

The Priest offers up the prayer of entrance,[1] *and for incense.*

The Priest.

O Sovereign Lord our God, who hast chosen the lamp of the twelve apostles with its twelve lights, and hast sent them forth to proclaim throughout the whole world and teach the gospel of Thy kingdom, and to heal sickness and every weakness among the people, and hast breathed upon their faces and said unto them, "Receive the Holy Spirit the Comforter: whosesoever sins ye remit, they are remitted unto them; and whosesoever sins ye retain, they are retained:" Breathe also

[1] This is the "little entrance."

Thy Holy Spirit upon us Thy servants, who, standing around, are about to enter on Thy holy service, [bestowing what is meet][1] upon the bishops, elders, deacons, readers, singers, and laity, with the entire body of the holy catholic and apostolic church. From the curse and execration, from condemnation, imprisonment, and banishment, and from the portion of the adversary, O Lord, deliver us. Purify our lives and cleanse our hearts from all pollution and from all wickedness, that with pure heart and conscience we may offer to Thee this incense for a sweet-smelling savour, and for the remission of our sins and the sins of all Thy people, through the grace, mercy, and love of Thine only-begotten Son.

Aloud.

Through whom and with whom be the glory and the power to Thee, with Thy all-holy, good, and life-giving Spirit, now, henceforth, and for evermore.

The People.

Amen.

The Deacon.

V. Stand.

They sing the " Only-begotten Son and Word." [2]

The Gospel is carried in, and the Deacon says:

Let us pray.

The Priest.

Peace be to all.

The People.

And to thy spirit.

The Deacon.

Let us pray.

---

[1] The text here is defective. Some suppose that a sentence has been lost.

[2] Given in full in c. VI. of the Liturgy of James.

The People.

Lord, have mercy.

The Priest says the prayer of the Trisagion.

O Sovereign Lord Christ Jesus, the co-eternal Word of the eternal Father, who wast made in all things like as we are, but without sin, for the salvation of our race; who hast sent forth Thy holy disciples and apostles to proclaim and teach the gospel of Thy kingdom, and to heal all disease, all sickness among Thy people, be pleased now, O Lord, to send forth Thy light and Thy truth. Enlighten the eyes of our minds, that we may understand Thy divine oracles. Fit us to become hearers, and not only hearers, but doers of Thy word, that we, becoming fruitful, and yielding good fruit from thirty to an hundred fold, may be deemed worthy of the kingdom of heaven.

Aloud.

Let Thy mercy speedily overtake us, O Lord. For Thou art the bringer of good tidings, the Saviour and Guardian of our souls and bodies; and we offer glory, thanks, and the *Trisagion* to Thee, the Father, Son, and Holy Ghost, now, henceforth, and for evermore.

The People.

Amen.
Holy God, holy mighty, holy immortal.

VI. *After the Trisagion the Priest makes the sign of the cross upon the people, and says:*
Peace be to all.

The People.

And to thy spirit.

Then follow the πρόσχωμεν (let us attend); The Apostle and Prologue of the Hallelujah. The Deacons, after a prescribed form, say:
Lord, bless us.[1]

[1] See note on p. 13.

The Priest says:

May the Lord in His mercy bless and help us, now, henceforth, and for evermore.

The Priest, before the Gospel is read, offers incense, and says:

Accept at Thy holy, heavenly, and reasonable altar, O Lord, the incense we offer in presence of Thy sacred glory. Send down upon us in return the grace of Thy Holy Spirit, for Thou art blessed, and let Thy glory encircle us.

VII. *The Deacon, when he is about to read the Gospel, says:*

Lord, bless us.

The Priest.

May the Lord, who is the blessed God, bless and strengthen us, and make us hearers of His holy Gospel, now, henceforth, and for evermore. Amen.

The Deacon.

Stand and let us hear the holy Gospel.

The Priest.

Peace be to all.

The People.

And to thy spirit.

VIII. *The Deacon reads the Gospel, and the Priest says the prayer of the Collect (τὴν συνάπτην).*

Look down in mercy and compassion, O Lord, and heal the sick among Thy people. May all our brethren who have gone or who are about to go abroad, safely reach their destination in due season. Send down the gracious rain upon the thirsty lands, and make the rivers flow in full stream, according to Thy grace. The fruits of the land do Thou, O Lord, fill with seed and make ripe for the harvest. In peace, courage, justice, and tranquillity preserve the kingdom of Thy servant, whom Thou hast deemed worthy to reign over this land. From evil days, from famine and pestilence, from the assault of barbarians, defend, O Lord, this Christ-loving city, lowly and worthy of Thy compassion, as Thou didst spare Nineveh of old; for Thou art full of mercy and compassion, and rememberest not the iniquities of men against them. Thou hast said through Thy prophet Isaiah, "I will defend this city, to save it for mine own sake, and for my servant David's sake." Wherefore we pray and beseech Thee to defend in Thy good mercy this city, for the sake of the martyr and evangelist Mark, who has shown us the way of salvation through the grace, mercy, and love of Thine only-begotten Son.

Aloud.

Through whom and with whom be glory and power to Thee, with Thy all-holy, good, and life-giving Spirit.

The Deacon.

IX. Begin.

Then they say the verse. The Deacon says the three.[1]

The Priest.

O Sovereign and Almighty God, the Father of our Lord Jesus Christ, we pray and beseech Thee to fill our hearts with the peace of heaven, and to bestow moreover the peace of this life. Preserve for us through many years our most holy and blessed Pope Δ [Patriarch], and our most pious Bishop Δ, while they, according to Thy holy and blessed will, peacefully fulfil the holy priesthood committed to their care, and dispense aright the word of truth, with all the orthodox bishops, elders, deacons, sub-deacons, readers, singers, with the entire body of the holy catholic and apostolic church. Bless our meetings, O Lord. Grant that we may hold them without let or hindrance, according to Thy holy will. Be pleased to give to us, and Thy servants after us for ever, houses of praise and prayer. Rise, O Lord, and

---

[1] Probably by *the three* are meant three prayers.

THE DIVINE LITURGY OF MARK. 55

let Thine enemies be scattered. Let all who hate Thy holy name be put to flight. Bless Thy faithful and orthodox people. Multiply them by thousands and tens of thousands.

Let no deadly sin prevail against them, or against Thy holy people, through the grace, mercy, and love of Thine only-begotten Son.

Aloud.

Through whom and with whom be glory and power to Thee, with Thy all-holy, good, and life-giving Spirit.

The People.

Amen.

The Priest.

Peace be to all.

The People.

And to thy spirit.

The Deacon.

Take care that none of the catechumens—[1]

Then they sing "The Cherubim" mystically.

X. *The Priest offers incense at the entrance, and prays:*

O Lord our God, who lackest nothing, accept this incense offered by an unworthy hand, and deem us all worthy of Thy blessing, for Thou art our sanctification, and we ascribe glory to Thee.

The holy things are carried to the altar, and the Priest prays thus:

O holy, highest, awe-inspiring God, who dwellest among the saints, sanctify us, and deem us worthy of Thy reverend priesthood. Bring us to Thy precious altar with a good conscience, and cleanse our hearts from all pollution. Drive away from us all unholy thoughts, and sanctify our souls and minds. Grant that, with reverence of Thee, we may perform the service of our holy fathers, and propitiate Thy

[1] Some such word as "remain" is intentionally omitted.

presence through all time; for Thou art He who blesseth and sanctifieth all things, and to Thee we ascribe glory and thanks.

The Deacon.

XI. Salute one another.

The Priest says the prayer of salutation.

O Sovereign and Almighty Lord, look down from heaven on Thy church, on all Thy people, and on all Thy flock. Save us all, Thy unworthy servants, the sheep of Thy fold. Give us Thy peace, Thy help, and Thy love, and send to us the gift of Thy Holy Spirit, that with a pure heart and a good conscience we may salute one another with an holy kiss, without hypocrisy, and with no hostile purpose, but guileless and pure in one spirit, in the bond of peace and love, one body and one spirit, in one faith, even as we have been called in one hope of our calling, that we may all meet in the divine and boundless love, in Christ Jesus our Lord, with whom Thou art blessed.

Then the Priest offers the incense, and says:

The incense is offered to Thy name. Let it ascend, we implore Thee, from the hands of Thy poor and sinful servants to Thy heavenly altar for a sweet-smelling savour, and the propitiation of all Thy people. For all glory, honour, adoration, and thanks are due unto Thee, the Father, Son, and Holy Ghost, now, henceforth, and for evermore. Amen.

After the " salutation," the Deacon in a loud voice says:

XII. Stand and make the offering duly.

The Priest, making the sign of the cross over the disks and chalices, says in a loud voice:

I believe in one God, etc.

The Deacon.

Stand for prayer.

The Priest.
Peace be to all.

The Deacon.
Pray for those who present the offering.

The Priest says the prayer of oblation (τῆς προθέσεως).

O Sovereign Lord, Christ Jesus the Word, who art equal in power with the Father and the Holy Spirit, the great high priest; the bread that came down from heaven, and saved our souls from ruin; who gavest Thyself, a spotless Lamb, for the life of the world: we pray and beseech Thee, O Lord, in Thy mercy, to let Thy presence rest upon this bread and these chalices on the all-holy table, while angels, archangels, and Thy holy priests stand round and minister for Thy glory and the renewing of our souls, through the grace, mercy, and love of Thine only-begotten Son, through whom and with whom be glory and power to Thee.

And when the People say,
And from the Holy Spirit was He made flesh;

The Priest makes the sign of the cross, and says:
And was crucified for us.

The Priest makes the sign of the cross again, and says:
And to the Holy Spirit.

XIII. *In like manner also, after the Creed, he makes the sign of the cross upon the people, and says aloud:*
The Lord be with all.

The People.
And with thy spirit.

The Priest.
Let us lift up our hearts.

The People.

We lift them up to the Lord.

The Priest.

Let us give thanks to the Lord.

The People.

It is meet and right.

The Deacon.

. . . . .

The Priest begins the Anaphora.

O Lord God, Sovereign and Almighty Father, truly it is meet and right, holy and becoming, and good for our souls, to praise, bless, and thank Thee; to make open confession to Thee by day and night with voice, lips, and heart without ceasing; to Thee who hast made the heaven, and all that is therein; the earth, and all that is therein; the sea, fountains, rivers, lakes, and all that is therein; to Thee who, after Thine own image and likeness, hast made man, upon whom Thou didst also bestow the joys of Paradise; and when he trespassed against Thee, Thou didst neither neglect nor forsake him, good Lord, but didst recall him by Thy law, instruct him by Thy prophets, restore and renew him by this awful, life-giving, and heavenly mystery. And all this Thou hast done by Thy wisdom and the light of truth, Thine only-begotten Son, our Lord, God, and Saviour Jesus Christ, through whom, thanking Thee with Him and the Holy Spirit, we offer this reasonable and bloodless sacrifice, which all nations, from the rising to the setting of the sun, from the north and the south, present to Thee, O Lord; for great is Thy name among all peoples, and in all places are incense, sacrifice, and oblation offered to Thy holy name.

XIV. We pray and beseech Thee, O Lord, to remember in Thy good mercy the holy and only catholic and apostolic church throughout the whole world, and all Thy people, and all the sheep of this fold. Vouchsafe to the hearts of all of us the peace of heaven, but grant us also the peace of this life.

Guide and direct in all peace the king [or emperor], army, magistrates, councils,[1] peoples, and neighbourhoods, and all our outgoings and incomings.

O King of Peace, grant us Thy peace in unity and love. May we be Thine, O Lord; for we know no other God but Thee, and name no other name but Thine. Give life unto the souls of all of us, and let no deadly sin prevail against us, or against all Thy people.

Look down in mercy and compassion, O Lord, and heal the sick among Thy people. Deliver them and us, O Lord, from sickness and disease, and drive away the spirit of weakness. Raise up those who have been long afflicted, and heal those who are vexed with unclean spirits. Have mercy on all who are in prison, or in mines, or on trial, or condemned, or in exile, or crushed by cruel bondage or tribute. Deliver them, O Lord, for Thou art our God, who settest the captives free; who raisest up the down-trodden; who givest hope to the hopeless, and help to the helpless; who liftest up the fallen; who givest refuge to the shipwrecked, and vengeance to the oppressed. Pity, relieve, and restore every Christian soul that is afflicted or wandering. But do Thou, O Lord, the physician of our souls and bodies, the guardian of all flesh, look down, and by Thy saving power heal all the diseases of soul and body. Guide and prosper our brethren who have gone or who are about to go abroad. Whether they travel by land, or river, or lake, by public road, or in whatever way journeying, bring them everywhere to a safe and tranquil haven. Be pleased to be with them by land and sea, and restore them in health and joy to joyful and healthful homes. Ever defend, O Lord, our journey through this life from trouble and storm. Send down rich and copious showers on the dry and thirsty lands. Gladden and revive the face of the earth, that it may spring forth and rejoice in the raindrops. Make the rivers flow in full stream.

Gladden and revive the face of the earth with the swelling waters. Fill all the channels of the streams, and multiply the fruits of the earth. Bless, O Lord, the fruits of the

---
[1] βουλάς, senates.

earth, and keep them safe and unharmed. Fill them with seed, and make them ripe for the harvest. Bless even now, O Lord, Thy yearly crown of blessing for the sake of the poor of Thy people, the widow, the orphan, and the stranger, and for the sake of all of us who have our hope in Thee and call upon Thy holy name; for the eyes of all are upon Thee, and Thou givest them bread in due season. O Thou who givest food to all flesh, fill our hearts with joy and gladness, that at all times, having all sufficiency, we may abound to every good work in Christ Jesus our Lord. O King of kings and Lord of lords, defend the kingdom of Thy servant, our orthodox and Christ-loving sovereign, whom Thou hast deemed worthy to reign over this land in peace, courage, and justice. Subdue under him, O Lord, every enemy and adversary, whether at home or abroad. Gird on Thy shield and armour, and rise to his aid. Draw Thy sword, and help him to fight against them that persecute him. Shield him in the day of battle, and grant that the fruit of his loins may sit upon his throne. Be kind to him, O Lord, for the sake of Thy holy and apostolic church, and all Thy Christ-loving people, that we too in his peaceful reign may live a calm and tranquil life, in all reverence and godliness. O Lord our God, give peace to the souls of our fathers and brethren who have fallen asleep in Jesus, remembering our forefathers of old, our fathers, patriarchs, prophets, apostles, martyrs, confessors, bishops, and the souls of all the holy and just men who have died in the Lord. Especially remember those whose memory we this day celebrate, and our holy father Mark, the apostle and evangelist, who has shown us the way of salvation.

Hail! thou art highly favoured; the Lord is with thee; blessed art thou among women, and blessed is the fruit of thy womb, because thou hast brought forth the Saviour of our souls.

Aloud.

Especially (remember) our all-holy, pure, and blessed Lady, Mary the Virgin Mother of God.

The Deacon.

Lord, bless us.

The Priest.

The Lord will bless thee in His grace, now, henceforth, and for evermore.

The Deacon reads the record of the dead (τὰ δίπτυχα).

The Priest bows and prays.

XV. Give peace, O Sovereign Lord our God, to the souls of all who dwell in the tabernacles of Thy saints. Graciously bestow upon them in Thy kingdom Thy promised blessing, which eye hath not seen, and ear hath not heard, nor has it entered into the heart of man what Thou, O God, hast prepared for those who love Thy holy name. Give peace to their souls, and deem them worthy of the kingdom of heaven. Grant that we may end our lives as Christians, acceptable unto Thee and without sin, and be pleased to give us part and lot with all Thy saints. Accept, O God, by Thy ministering archangels at Thy holy, heavenly, and reasonable altar in the spacious heavens, the thankofferings of those who offer sacrifice and oblation, and of those who desire to offer much or little, in secret or openly, but have it not to give. Accept the thankofferings of those who have presented them this day, as Thou didst accept the gifts of Thy righteous Abel.

The Priest offers incense, and says:

As Thou didst accept the sacrifice of our father Abraham, the incense of Zacharias, the alms of Cornelius, and the widow's two mites, accept also the thankofferings of these, and give them for the things of time the things of eternity, and for the things of earth the things of heaven. Defend, O Lord, our most holy and blessed Pope [Patriarch] Δ, whom Thou hast fore-ordained to rule over Thy holy catholic and apostolic church, and our most pious Bishop Δ, that they through many years of peace may, according to Thy holy and blessed will, fulfil the sacred priesthood committed to their care, and dispense aright the word of truth. Remember the orthodox bishops everywhere, the elders, deacons, sub-deacons, readers, singers, monks, virgins, widows, and laity. Remember, O Lord, the holy city of our God, Jesus Christ, and the imperial city, and this city of ours, and all cities and all lands, and the peace and safety of those who dwell therein in the orthodox faith of Christ. Be mindful, O Lord, of the return of the backsliding, and of every Christian soul that is afflicted and oppressed, and in need of Thy divine mercy and help. Be mindful, O Lord, of our brethren in captivity. Grant that they may find mercy and compassion with those who have led them captive. Be mindful also of us, O Lord, Thy sinful and unworthy servants, and blot out our sins in Thy goodness and mercy. Be mindful also of me, Thy lowly, sinful, and unworthy servant, and in Thy mercy blot out my sins. Be with us, O Lord, who minister unto Thy holy name. Bless our meetings, O Lord. Utterly uproot idolatry from the world. Crush under our feet Satan, and all his wicked influence. Humble now, as at all times, the enemies of Thy church. Lay bare their pride. Speedily show them their weakness. Bring to nought the wicked plots they contrive against us. Arise, O Lord, and let Thine enemies be scattered, and let all who hate Thy holy name be put to flight. Do Thou bless a thousand times ten thousand Thy faithful and orthodox people while they do Thy holy will.

The Deacon.

Let those who are seated stand.

The Priest says the following prayer:

Deliver the captive; rescue the distressed; feed the hungry; comfort the faint-hearted; convert the erring; enlighten the darkened; raise the fallen; confirm the wavering; heal the sick; and guide them all, good Lord, into the way of salvation, and into Thy sacred fold. Deliver us from our iniquities; protect and defend us at all times.

The Deacon.

Turn to the east.

The Priest bows and prays.

For Thou art far above all principality, and power, and might, and dominion, and every name that is named, not only in this world, but in that which is to come. Round Thee stand ten thousand times ten thousand, and thousands of thousands of holy angels and hosts of archangels; and Thy two most honoured creatures, the many-eyed cherubim and the six-winged seraphim. With twain they cover their faces, and with twain they cover their feet, and with twain they do fly; and they cry one to another for ever with the voice of praise, and glorify Thee, O Lord, singing aloud the triumphal and thrice-holy[1] hymn to Thy great glory.

Holy, holy, holy, Lord God of Sabaoth. Heaven and earth are full of Thy glory:

Aloud.

Thou dost ever sanctify all men; but with all who glorify Thee, receive also, O Sovereign Lord, our sanctification, who with them celebrate Thy praise, and say,

The People.

Holy, holy, holy Lord.

The Priest makes the sign of the cross over the sacred mysteries.

XVI. For truly heaven and earth are full of Thy glory, through the manifestation of our Lord and God and Saviour Jesus Christ. Fill, O God, this sacrifice with Thy blessing, through the inspiration of Thy all-holy Spirit. For the Lord Himself, our God and universal King, Christ Jesus, reclining at meat the same night on which he delivered Himself up for our sins and died in the flesh for all, took bread in His holy, pure, and guiltless hands, and lifting His eyes to His Father, our God, and the God of all, gave thanks; and when He had blessed, hallowed, and broken the bread, gave it to His holy and blessed disciples and apostles, saying,

---

[1] The Trisagion.

Aloud.

"Take, eat."

The Deacon.

Pray earnestly.

The Priest (aloud).

For this is my body, which is broken for you, and divided for the remission of sins.

The People.

Amen.

The Priest prays.

After the same manner also, when He had supped, He took the cup of wine mingled with water, and lifting His eyes to Thee, His Father, our God, and the God of all, gave thanks; and when He had blessed and filled it with the Holy Spirit, gave it to His holy and blessed disciples and apostles, saying,

Aloud.

Drink ye all of it.

The Deacon.

Pray earnestly again.

The Priest (aloud).

For this is my blood of the new testament, which is shed for you and for many, and distributed among you for the remission of sins.

The People.

Amen.

The Priest prays thus:

This do ye in remembrance of me; for as often as ye eat this bread and drink this cup, ye do show forth my death and acknowledge my resurrection and ascension until I come.

O Sovereign and Almighty Lord, King of heaven, while we show forth the death of Thine only-begotten Son, our Lord, God, and Saviour Jesus Christ, and acknowledge His blessed resurrection from the dead on the third day, we do also openly declare His ascension into heaven, and His sitting on the right hand of Thee, God and Father, and await His second terrible and dreadful coming, in which He will come to judge righteously the quick and the dead, and to render to each man according to his works.

XVII. O Lord our God, we have placed before Thee what is Thine from Thine own mercies. We pray and beseech Thee, O good and merciful God, to send down from Thy holy heaven, from the mansion Thou hast prepared, and from Thine infinite bosom, the Paraclete Himself, holy, powerful, and life-giving, the Spirit of truth, who spake in the law, the apostles, and prophets; who is everywhere present, and filleth all things, freely working sanctification in whom He will with Thy good pleasure; one in His nature; manifold in His working; the fountain of divine blessing; of like substance with Thee, and proceeding from Thee; sitting with Thee on the throne of Thy kingdom, and with Thine only-begotten Son, our Lord and God and Saviour Jesus Christ. Send down upon us also, and upon this bread and upon these cups, Thy Holy Spirit, that by His all-powerful and divine influence He may sanctify and consecrate them, and make this bread the body.

The People.

Amen.

The Priest (aloud).

And this cup the blood of the new testament, of the very Lord, and God, and Saviour, and universal King Christ Jesus.

The Deacon.

Deacons, come down.

The Priest (aloud).

That to all of us who partake thereof they may tend unto

faith, sobriety, healing, temperance, sanctification, the renewal of soul, body, and spirit, participation in the blessedness of eternal life and immortality, the glory of Thy most holy name, and the remission of sins, that Thy most holy, precious, and glorious name may be praised and glorified in this as in all things.

The People.

As it was and is.

The Priest.

XVIII. Peace be to all.

The Deacon.

Pray.

The Priest prays in secret.

O God of light, Father of life, Author of Grace, Creator of worlds, Founder of knowledge, Giver of wisdom, Treasure of holiness, Teacher of pure prayers, Benefactor of our souls, who givest to the faint-hearted who put their trust in Thee those things into which the angels desire to look. O Sovereign Lord, who hast brought us up from the depths of darkness to light, who hast given us life from death, who hast graciously bestowed upon us freedom from slavery, who hast scattered the darkness of sin within us, through the presence of Thine only-begotten Son, do Thou now also, through the visitation of Thy all-holy Spirit, enlighten the eyes of our understanding, that we may partake without fear of condemnation of this heavenly and immortal food, and sanctify us wholly in soul, body, and spirit, that with Thy holy disciples and apostles we may say this prayer to Thee: "Our Father who art in heaven," etc.

Aloud.

And grant, O Sovereign Lord, in Thy mercy, that we with freedom of speech, without fear of condemnation, with pure heart and enlightened soul, with face that is not ashamed, and with hallowed lips, may venture to call upon Thee, the holy God who art in heaven, as our Father, and say:

The People.

Our Father who art in heaven, etc.

The Priest prays.

Verily, Lord, Lord, lead us not into temptation, but deliver us from evil; for Thy abundant mercy showeth that we through our great infirmity are unable to resist it. Grant that we may find a way whereby we may be able to withstand temptation; for Thou hast given us power to tread upon serpents, and scorpions, and all the power of the enemy.

Aloud.

For Thine is the kingdom and power.

The People.

Amen.

The Priest.

XIX. Peace be to all.

The Deacon.

Bow your heads to Jesus.

The People.

Thou, Lord.

The Priest prays.

O Sovereign and Almighty Lord, who sittest upon the cherubim, and art glorified by the seraphim; who hast made the heaven out of waters, and adorned it with choirs of stars; who hast placed an unbodied host of angels in the highest heavens to sing Thy praise for ever; before Thee have we bowed our souls and bodies in token of our bondage. We beseech Thee to repel the dark assaults of sin from our understanding, and to gladden our minds with the divine radiance of Thy Holy Spirit, that, filled with the knowledge of Thee, we may worthily partake of the mercies set before us, the pure body and precious blood of Thine only-begotten Son, our Lord and God and Saviour Jesus Christ. Pardon all our sins in Thy abundant and unsearchable goodness, through the grace, mercy, and love of Thine only-begotten Son.

Aloud.

Through whom and with whom be glory and power to Thee, with the all-holy, good, and life-giving Spirit.

The Priest.

XX. Peace be to all.

The Deacon.

With the fear of God.

The Priest prays.

O holy, highest, awe-inspiring God, who dwellest among the saints, sanctify us by the word of Thy grace and by the inspiration of Thy all-holy Spirit; for Thou hast said, O Lord our God, "Be ye holy; for I am holy." O Word of God, past finding out, consubstantial and co-eternal with the Father and the Holy Spirit, and sharer of their sovereignty, accept the pure song which cherubim and seraphim, and the unworthy lips of Thy sinful and unworthy servant, sing aloud.

The People.

Lord, have mercy; Lord, have mercy; Lord, have mercy.

The Priest (aloud).

Holy things for the holy.

The People.

One Father holy, one Son holy, one Spirit holy, in the unity of the Holy Spirit. Amen.

The Deacon.

For salvation and help.

The Priest makes the sign of the cross upon the people, and saith in a loud voice:

The Lord be with all.

The Priest breaks the bread, and saith:

Praise ye God.

The Priest divides it among those present, and saith:

The Lord will bless and help you through His great (mercy).

The Priest says:

Command.

The Clergy say:

The Holy Spirit commands and sanctifies.

The Priest.

Lo, they are sanctified and consecrated.

The Clergy.

One Father holy (*thrice*).

The Priest says:

The Lord be with all.

The Clergy.

And with thy spirit.

The Priest says:

The Lord Himself hath blessed it.

The Priest partakes, and prays.

" According to Thy loving-kindness," etc.

Or,

" As the hart panteth after the water-brooks," etc.

When he gives the bread to the clergy, he says:

The holy body.

And when he gives the chalice, he says:
The precious blood of our Lord, and God, and Saviour.

After the service is completed, the Deacon says:
XXI. Stand for prayer.

The Priest.
Peace be to all.

The Deacon.
Pray.

The Priest says the prayer of thanksgiving.

O Sovereign Lord our God, we thank Thee that we have partaken of Thy holy, pure, immortal, and heavenly mysteries, which Thou hast given for our good, and for the sanctification and salvation of our souls and bodies. We pray and beseech Thee, O Lord, to grant in Thy good mercy, that by partaking of the holy body and precious blood of Thine only-begotten Son, we may have faith that is not ashamed, love that is unfeigned, fulness of holiness, power to eschew evil and keep Thy commandments, provision for eternal life, and an acceptable defence before the awful tribunal of Thy Christ.

In a loud voice.

Through whom and with whom be glory and power to Thee, with Thy all-holy, good, and life-giving Spirit.

The Priest then turns to the people, and says:

XXII. O mightiest King, co-eternal with the Father, who by Thy might hast vanquished hell and trodden death under foot, who hast bound the strong man, and by Thy miraculous power and the enlightening radiance of Thy unspeakable Godhead hast raised Adam from the tomb, send forth Thy invisible right hand, which is full of blessing, and bless us all. Pity us, O Lord, and strengthen us by Thy divine power. Take away from us the sinful and wicked influence of carnal desire. Let the light shine into our souls, and dispel the surrounding darkness of sin. Unite us to the all-blessed assembly that is well-pleasing unto Thee; for through Thee and with Thee, all praise, honour, power, adoration, and thanksgiving are due unto the Father and the Holy Spirit, now, henceforth, and for evermore.

The Deacon.

Depart in peace.

The People.

In the name of the Lord.

The Priest (aloud).

XXIII. The love of God the Father; the grace of the Son, our Lord Jesus Christ; the communion and gift of the all-holy Spirit, be with us all, now, henceforth, and for evermore.

The People.

Amen. Blessed be the name of the Lord.

The Priest prays in the sacristy, and says :

O Lord, Thou hast given us sanctification by partaking of the all-holy body and precious blood of Thine only-begotten Son; give us the grace and gift of the all-holy Spirit. Enable us to lead blameless lives; and guide us unto the perfect redemption, and adoption, and the everlasting joys of the world to come. For Thou art our sanctification, and we ascribe glory unto Thee, the Father, and the Son, and the all-holy Spirit, now, henceforth, and for evermore.

The People.

Amen.

The Priest.

Peace be to all.

The People.

And to thy spirit.

The Priest dismisses them, and says :

May God bless, who blesseth and sanctifieth, who defendeth and preserveth us all through the partaking of His holy mysteries; and who is blessed for ever. Amen.

III.
LITURGY OF THE HOLY APOSTLES,
OR ORDER OF THE SACRAMENTS.

I. *First:* Glory to God in the highest; *and,* Our Father which art in heaven.

Prayer.

Strengthen, O our Lord and God, our weakness through Thy mercy, that we may administer the holy mystery which has been given for the renovation and salvation of our degraded nature, through the mercies of Thy beloved Son the Lord of all.

On common days.

Adored, glorified, lauded, celebrated, exalted, and blessed in heaven and on earth, be the adorable and glorious name of Thine ever-glorious Trinity, O Lord of all.

On common days they sing the Psalm (xv.), Lord, who shall dwell in Thy tabernacle? *entire with its canon,*[1] *of the mystery of the sacraments.*

Aloud.

Who shall shout with joy?

Prayer.

II. Before the resplendent throne of Thy majesty, O Lord, and the exalted and sublime throne of Thy glory, and on the

---

[1] Suicer says that a canon is a psalm or hymn (*canticum*) wont to be sung on certain days, ordinarily and as if by rule. He quotes Zonaras, who says that a canon is metrical, and is composed of nine odes. See Sophocles, *Glossary of Byzantine Greek*, Introduction, § 43. The canon of the Nestorian Church is somewhat different. See Neale, *General Introduction to the History of the Eastern Church*, p. 979.

awful seat of the strength of Thy love and the propitiatory altar which Thy will hath established, in the region of Thy pasture, with thousands of cherubim praising Thee, and ten thousands of seraphim sanctifying Thee, we draw near, adore, thank, and glorify Thee always, O Lord of all.

On commemorations and Fridays.

Thy name, great and holy, illustrious and blessed, the blessed and incomprehensible name of Thy glorious Trinity, and Thy kindness to our race, we ought at all times to bless, adore, and glorify, O Lord of all.

Responsory[1] *at the chancel, as above.*

Who commanded. To the priest. How breathes in us, O our Lord and God, the sweet fragrance of the sweetness of Thy love; illumined are our souls, through the knowledge of Thy truth: may we be rendered worthy of receiving the manifestation of Thy beloved from Thy holy heavens: there shall we render thanks unto Thee, and (in the meantime) glorify Thee without ceasing in Thy church, crowned and filled with every aid and blessing, because Thou art Lord and Father, Creator of all.

III. *Prayer of incense.*

We shall repeat the hymn to Thy glorious Trinity, O Father, Son, and Holy Ghost.

On fast-days.

And on account.

At the commemoration of saints.

Thou, O Lord, art truly the raiser up of our bodies: Thou art the good Saviour of our souls, and the secure preserver of our life; and we ought to thank Thee continually, to adore and glorify Thee, O Lord of all.

---

[1] "The psalm, or verses of a psalm, sung after the epistle, was always entitled *gradual*, from being chanted on the steps (*gradus*) of the pulpit. When sung by one person without interruption, it was called *tractus*; when chanted alternately by several singers, it was termed *responsory*."—PALMER, *Origines Liturgicæ*, vol. ii. p. 46, note.

At the lessons.[1]

Holy art Thou, worthy of praise, mighty, immortal, who dwellest in the holies, and Thy will resteth in them : have regard unto us, O Lord ; be merciful unto us, and pity us, as Thou art our helper in all circumstances, O Lord of all.

IV. *At the apostle.*[2]

Enlighten, O our Lord and God, the movements of our meditations to hear and understand the sweet listenings to Thy life-giving and divine commands; and grant unto us through Thy grace and mercy to gather from them the assurance of love, and hope, and salvation suitable to soul and body, and we shall sing to Thee everlasting glory without ceasing and always, O Lord of all.

On fast-days.

To Thee, the wise governor.

V. *Descending, he shall salute the Gospel, saying this prayer before the altar.*

Thee, the renowned seed of Thy Father, and the image of the person of Thy Father, who wast revealed in the body of our humanity, and didst arise to us in the light of Thy annunciation, Thee we thank, adore, etc.

And after the proclamation :[3]

Thee, O Lord God Almighty, we beseech and entreat, perfect with us Thy grace, and pour out through our hands Thy gift, the pity and compassion of Thy divinity. May they be to us for the propitiation of the offences of Thy people, and for the forgiveness of the sins of the entire flock of Thy pasture, through Thy grace and tender mercies, O good friend of men, O Lord of all.

VI. *The Deacons say :*

Bow your heads.

---

[1] *i.e.* while the lesson from the Old Testament is being read.

[2] *i.e.* while the lesson from the Apostolical Epistles is being read.

[3] Renaudot understands by the proclamation the reading aloud of the Gospel.

The Priest says this secret prayer in the sanctuary (Bema):

O Lord God Omnipotent, Thine is the holy catholic church, inasmuch as Thou, through the great passion of Thy Christ, didst buy the sheep of Thy pasture; and from the grace of the Holy Spirit, who is indeed of one nature with Thy glorious divinity, are granted the degrees of the true priestly ordination; and through Thy clemency Thou didst vouchsafe, O Lord, to make our weakness spiritual members in the great body of Thy holy church, that we might administer spiritual aid to faithful souls. Now, O Lord, perfect Thy grace with us, and pour out Thy gift through our hands: and may Thy tender mercies and the clemency of Thy divinity be upon us, and upon the people whom Thou hast chosen for Thyself.

Aloud.

And grant unto us, O Lord, through Thy clemency, that we may all together, and equally every day of our life, please Thy divinity, and be rendered worthy of the aid of Thy grace to offer Thee praise, honour, thanksgiving, and adoration at all times, O Lord.

VII. *And the Deacons ascend to the altar, and say:*

He who has not received baptism, etc.[1]

And the Priest begins the responsory of the mysteries, and the Sacristan and Deacon place the disk and the chalice upon the altar. The Priest crosses his hands, and says:

We offer praise to Thy glorious Trinity at all times and for ever.

And proceeds:

May Christ, who was offered for our salvation, and commanded us to commemorate His death and His resurrection, Himself receive this sacrifice from the hands of our weakness, through His grace and mercies for ever. Amen.

[1] The Malabar Lit. fills up, "let him depart."

And proceeds:

Laid are the renowned holy and life-giving mysteries upon the altar of the mighty Lord, even until His advent, for ever. Amen.

Praise. Thy memory. Our Father. The apostles of the Father. Upon the holy altar. They who have slept. Matthew, Mark, Luke, etc.

THE LITURGY OF THE BLESSED APOSTLES,

COMPOSED BY ST. ADÆUS AND ST. MARIS, TEACHERS OF THE EASTERNS.[1]

VIII. *The Priest draws near to celebrate, and thrice bows before the altar, the middle of which he kisses, then the right and the left wings; and bows to the higher portion of it, and says:*

Bless, O Lord. Pray for me, my fathers, brethren, and masters, that God may grant unto me the capability and power to perform this service to which I have drawn near, and that this oblation may be accepted from the hands of my weakness, for myself, for you, and for the whole body of the holy catholic church, through His grace and mercies for ever. Amen.

And they respond:

May Christ listen to thy prayers, and be pleased with thy sacrifice, receive thy oblation, and honour thy priesthood, and grant unto us, through thy mediation, the pardon of our offences, and the forgiveness of our sins, through His grace and mercies for ever.

Presently he bows to the lower part, uttering the same words; and they respond in the same manner: then he bows to the altar, and says:

God, Lord of all, be with us all through His grace and mercies for ever. Amen.

---

[1] "In the Syriac copy, 70, *Biblioth. Reg.*, this title does not occur, the service going forward without interruption."—ETHERIDGE.

And bowing to the Deacon, who is on the left, he says:

God, the Lord of all, confirm thy words, and secure to thee peace, and accept this oblation from my hands for me, for thee, for the whole body of the holy catholic church, and for the entire world, through His grace and mercies for ever.

He bows himself to the altar, and says in secret:

IX. O our Lord and God, look not on the multitude of our sins, and let not Thy dignity be turned away on account of the heinousness of our iniquities; but through Thine unspeakable grace sanctify this sacrifice of Thine, and grant through it power and capability, so that Thou mayest forget our many sins, and be merciful when Thou shalt appear at the end of time, in the man whom Thou hast assumed from among us, and we may find before Thee grace and mercy, and be rendered worthy to praise Thee with spiritual[1] assemblies.

He rises, and says this prayer in secret:

We thank Thee, O our Lord and God, for the abundant riches of Thy grace to us.

And he proceeds:

Us who were sinful and degraded, on account of the multitude of Thy clemency, Thou hast made worthy to celebrate the holy mysteries of the body and blood of Thy Christ. We beg aid from Thee for the strengthening of our souls, that in perfect love and true faith we may administer Thy gift to us.

Canon.

And we shall ascribe to Thee praise, glory, thanksgiving, and adoration, now, always, and for ever and ever.

He signs himself with the sign of the cross, and they respond:

Amen.

X. *And he proceeds:*

Peace be with you.

[1] Intellectualibus.

They respond:
With thee and with thy spirit.

And they give peace to each other, and say:
For all [Catholics].[1]

The Deacon says:
Let us thank, entreat, and beseech.

The priest says this prayer in secret:
O Lord, mighty God, help my weakness through Thy clemency and the aid of Thy grace; and make me worthy of offering before Thee this oblation, as for the common aid of all, and to the praise of Thy Trinity, O Father, Son, and Holy Ghost.

Another prayer, which is said also in the Liturgy of Nestorius.
O our Lord and God, restrain our thoughts, that they wander not amid the vanities of this world. O Lord our God, grant that I may be united to the affection of Thy love, unworthy though I be. Glory be to Thee, O Christ.

Ascend into the chamber of Thy renowned light, O Lord; sow in me the good seed of humility; and under the wings of Thy grace hide me through Thy mercy. If Thou wert to mark iniquities, O Lord, who shall stand? Because there is mercy with Thee.

In another MS. *the Priest says the following prayer in secret:*
O mother of our Lord Jesus Christ, beseech for me the only-begotten Son, who was born of thee, to forgive me my offences and my sins, and to accept from my feeble and sinful hands this sacrifice which my weakness offers upon this altar, through thy intercession for me, O holy mother.

XI. *When the Deacon shall say,* With watchfulness and care, *immediately the Priest rises up and uncovers the sacraments, taking away the veil with which they were covered: he blesses the incense, and says a canon with a loud voice.*

The grace of our Lord Jesus Christ, and the love of God

---
[1] The word Catholics is omitted in most MSS.

the Father, and the communion of the Holy Ghost, be with us all, now, etc.

He signs the sacraments, and they respond:

Amen.

The Priest proceeds:

Upwards be your minds.

They respond:

They are towards Thee, O God of Abraham, Isaac, and Israel, O glorious King.

The Priest.

The oblation is offered to God, the Lord of all.

They respond:

It is meet and right.

The Deacon.

Peace be with you.

The Priest puts on the incense, and says this prayer:

O Lord, Lord, grant me an open countenance before Thee, that with the confidence which is from Thee we may fulfil this awful and divine sacrifice with consciences free from all iniquity and bitterness. Sow in us, O Lord, affection, peace, and concord towards each other, and toward every one.

And standing, he says in secret:

Worthy of glory from every mouth, and of thanksgiving from all tongues, and of adoration and exaltation from all creatures, is the adorable and glorious name of Father, Son, and Holy Ghost, who created the world through His grace, and its inhabitants through His clemency, who saved men through His mercy, and showed great favour towards mortals. Thy majesty, O Lord, thousands of thousands of heavenly (spirits), and ten thousand myriads of holy angels, hosts of spirits, ministers of fire and spirit, bless and adore; with the holy cherubim and the spiritual seraphim they sanctify and celebrate Thy name, crying and praising, without ceasing crying unto each other.

They say with a loud voice:

Holy, holy, holy, Lord God Almighty; full are the heavens and the earth of His glory.

The Priest in secret:

Holy, holy, holy art Thou, O Lord God Almighty; the heavens and the earth are full of His glory and the nature of His essence, as they are glorious with the honour of His splendour; (as it is written), The heaven and the earth are full of me, saith the mighty Lord. Holy art Thou, O God [our] Father, truly the only one, of whom the whole family in heaven and earth is named. Holy art Thou, Eternal Son, through whom all things were made. Holy art Thou, holy, eternal Spirit, through whom all things are sanctified. Woe to me, woe to me, who have been astonied, because I am a man of polluted lips, and dwell among a people of polluted lips, and my eyes have seen the King, the mighty Lord. How terrible to-day is this place! For this is none other than the house of God and the gate of heaven; because Thou hast been seen eye to eye, O Lord. Now, I pray, may Thy grace be with us, O Lord; purge away our impurities, and sanctify our lips; unite the voices of our insignificance with the sanctification of seraphim and archangels. Glory be to Thy tender mercies, because Thou hast associated the earthly with the heavenly.[1]

And he proceeds, saying in secret this prayer, in a bowing posture:

XII. And with those heavenly powers we give Thee thanks, even we, Thine insignificant, pithless, and feeble servants; because Thou hast granted unto us Thy great grace which cannot be repaid. For indeed Thou didst take upon Thee our human nature, that Thou mightest bestow life on us through Thy divinity; Thou didst exalt our low condition;

[1] Spiritualibus.

Thou didst raise our ruined state; Thou didst rouse up our mortality; Thou didst wash away our sins; Thou didst blot out the guilt of our sins; Thou didst enlighten our intelligence, and Thou didst condemn our enemy, O Lord our God; and Thou didst cause the insignificance of our pithless nature to triumph. Through the tender mercies of Thy grace poured out, O clement One, pardon our offences and sins; blot out my offences in the judgment. And on account of all Thy aids and Thy favours to us, we shall ascribe unto Thee praise,[1] honour, thanksgiving, and adoration, now, always, and for ever and ever.

The Priest signs the sacraments. The response is made.

Amen.

The Deacon.

In your minds. Pray for peace with us.

The Priest says this prayer bowing, and in a low voice:

O Lord God Almighty, accept this oblation for the whole holy catholic church, and for all the pious and righteous fathers who have been pleasing to Thee, and for all the prophets and apostles, and for all the martyrs and confessors, and for all that mourn, that are in straits, and are sick, and for all that are under difficulties and trials, and for all the weak and the oppressed, and for all the dead that have gone from amongst us; then for all that ask a prayer from our weakness, and for me, a degraded and feeble sinner. O Lord our God, according to Thy mercies and the multitude of Thy favours, look upon Thy people, and on me, a feeble man, not according to my sins and my follies, but that they may become worthy of the forgiveness of their sins through this holy body, which they receive with faith, through the grace of Thy mercy for ever and ever. Amen.

In another MS. *that prayer begins thus:*

O Lord God Almighty, hear the voice of my cry before

---

[1] Hymnum.

Thee at this time. Give ear, O Lord, and hear my groanings before Thy majesty, and accept the entreaty of me, a sinner, with which I call upon Thy grace, at this hour at which the sacrifice is offered to Thy Father. Have mercy on all creatures; spare the guilty; convert the erring; restore the oppressed; on the disquieted bestow rest; heal the weak; console the afflicted; and perfect the alms of those who work righteousness on account of Thy holy name. Have mercy on me also, a sinner, through Thy grace. O Lord God Almighty, may this oblation be accepted for the entire holy catholic church; and for priests, kings, princes, *and the rest as above.*

The Priest says this prayer of inclination in secret:

XIII. Do Thou, O Lord, through Thy many and ineffable mercies, make the memorial good and acceptable to all the pious and righteous fathers who have been pleading before Thee in the commemoration of the body and blood of Thy Christ, which we offer to Thee upon Thy pure and holy altar, as Thou hast taught us; and grant unto us Thy rest all the days of this life.

He proceeds:

O Lord our God, bestow on us Thy rest and peace all the days of this life, that all the inhabitants of the earth may know Thee, that Thou art the only true God the Father, and Thou didst send our Lord Jesus Christ, Thy Son and Thy beloved; and He Himself our Lord and God came and taught us all purity and holiness. Make remembrance of prophets, apostles, martyrs, confessors, bishops, doctors, priests, deacons, and all the sons of the holy catholic church who have been signed with the sign of life, of holy baptism. We also, O Lord.

He proceeds:

We, Thy degraded, weak, and feeble servants who are congregated in Thy name, and now stand before Thee, and have received with joy the form which is from Thee, praising, glorifying, and exalting, commemorate and celebrate this great, awful, holy, and divine mystery of the passion, death, burial, and resurrection of our Lord and Saviour Jesus Christ.

And may Thy Holy Spirit come, O Lord, and rest upon this oblation of Thy servants which they offer, and bless and sanctify it; and may it be unto us, O Lord, for the propitiation of our offences and the forgiveness of our sins, and for a grand hope of resurrection from the dead, and for a new life in the kingdom of the heavens, with all who have been pleasing before Him. And on account of the whole of Thy wonderful dispensation towards us, we shall render thanks unto Thee, and glorify Thee without ceasing in Thy church, redeemed by the precious blood of Thy Christ, with open mouths and joyful countenances:

Canon.

Ascribing praise,[1] honour, thanksgiving, and adoration to Thy holy, loving, and life-giving name, now, always, and for ever.

The Priest signs the mysteries with the cross, and they respond:

Amen.

The Priest bows himself and kisses the altar, first in the midde, then at the two sides right and left, and says this prayer:

In another MS., says a Psalm.[2] Have mercy upon me, O God, *even to*, and sinners shall be converted unto Thee. Unto Thee lift I up mine eyes,[3] *even to*, have mercy upon us, O Lord, have mercy upon us. Stretch forth Thy hand, and let Thy right hand save me, O Lord; may Thy mercies remain upon me, O Lord, for ever, and despise not the works of Thy hands.

Then he says this prayer:

XIV. O Christ, peace of those in heaven and great rest of

[1] Hymnum.   [2] Ps. li.   [3] Ps. cxxiii.

those below,[1] grant that Thy rest and peace may dwell in the four parts of the world, but especially in Thy holy catholic church; grant that the priesthood with the government may have peace; cause wars to cease from the ends of the earth, and scatter the nations that delight in wars,[2] that we may enjoy the blessing of living in tranquillity and peace, in all temperance and fear of God. Spare the offences and sins of the dead, through Thy grace and mercies for ever.

And to those who are around the altar he says:

Bless, O Lord. Bless, O Lord.

And he puts on the incense with which he covers himself, and says:

Sweeten, O Lord our God, the pleasant odour of our souls through the sweetness of Thy love, and through it cleanse me from the stains of my sin, and forgive me my offences and sins, whether known or unknown to me.

A second time he takes the incense with both hands, and censes the mysteries; presently he says:

The clemency of Thy grace, O our Lord and God, gives us access to these renowned, holy, life-giving, and divine mysteries, unworthy though we be.

The Priest repeats these words once and again, and at each interval unites his hands over his breast in the form of a cross. He kisses the altar in the middle, and receives with both hands the upper oblation; and looking up, says:

Praise be to Thy holy name, O Lord Jesus Christ, and adoration to Thy majesty, always and for ever. Amen. For He is the living and life-giving bread which cometh down from heaven, and giveth life to the whole world, of which they who eat die not; and they who receive it are saved by it, and do not see corruption, and live through it for ever; and Thou art the antidote of our mortality, and the resurrection of our entire frame.

[1] *i.e.* the dead. [2] Lit. "wish for wars."

In another MS. *there is a different reading.*

Glory to Thee, O God the Father, who didst send Thine only-begotten Son for our salvation, and He Himself before He suffered, etc.

XV. *In the* MS. *of Elias, which we have followed, there is a defect, seeing that the whole recitation of the words of Christ is omitted through the fault of the transcriber, or because these ought to have been taken from another source, namely, from the Liturgy of Theodorus or Nestorius. In that which the Patriarch Joseph wrote at Rome,* 1697, *that entire passage is remodelled according to the Chaldean missal published at Rome, as in the mass, a translation of which was edited by Alexius Menesius. Since there were no other codices at hand, in this place it seemed good to place asterisks to indicate the defects.* * * * *

XVI. Praise to Thy holy name, O Lord,—*as above.*

The Priest kisses the host in the form of a cross; in such a way, however, that his lips do not touch it, but appear to kiss it; and he says:

Glory to Thee, O Lord; glory to Thee, O Lord, on account of Thine unspeakable gift to us, for ever.

Then he draws nigh to the fraction of the host, which he accomplishes with both his hands, saying:

We draw nigh, O Lord, with true faith, and break with thanksgiving and sign through Thy mercy the body and blood of our Life-giver, Jesus Christ, in the name of the Father, Son, and Holy Ghost.

And, naming the Trinity, he breaks the host, which he holds in his hands, into two parts: and the one which is in his left hand he lays down on the disk; with the other, which he holds in his right hand, he signs the chalice, saying:

The precious blood is signed with the holy body of our Lord Jesus Christ. In the name of the Father, and the Son, and the Holy Ghost for ever.

And they respond:

Amen.

Then he dips it even to the middle in the chalice, and signs with it the body which is in the paten, saying:

The holy body is signed with the propitiatory blood of our Lord Jesus Christ. In the name of the Father, and of the Son, and of the Holy Ghost for ever.

And they respond:

Amen.

And he unites the two parts, the one with the other, saying:

Divided, sanctified, completed, perfected, united, and commingled have been these renowned, holy, life-giving, and divine mysteries, the one with the other, in the adorable and glorious name of Thy glorious Trinity, O Father, Son, and Holy Ghost, that they may be to us, O Lord, for the propitiation of our offences and the forgiveness of our sins; also for the grand hope of a resurrection from the dead, and of a new life in the kingdom of the heavens, for us and for the holy church of Christ our Lord, here and in every place whatsoever, now and always, and for ever.

XVII. *In the meantime he signs the host with his right thumb in the form of a cross from the lower part to the upper, and from the right to the left, and thus forms a slight fissure in it where it has been dipped in the blood. He puts a part of it into the chalice in the form of a cross: the lower part is placed towards the priest, the upper towards the chalice, so that the place of the fissure looks to the chalice. He bows, and rising, says:*

Glory be to Thee, O Lord Jesus Christ, who hast made me, unworthy though I be, through Thy grace, a minister and mediator of Thy renowned, holy, life-giving, and divine mysteries: through the grace of Thy mercy, make me worthy of the pardon of my offences and the forgiveness of my sins.

He signs himself with the sign of the cross on his forehead, and does the same to those standing round him.

In another MS.

He signs his forehead with the sign of the cross, and says:

Glory to Thee, O Lord, who didst create me by Thy grace. Glory to Thee, O Lord, who didst call me by Thy mercy. Glory to Thee, O Lord, who didst appoint me the mediator of Thy gift; and on account of all the benefits to my weakness, ascribed unto Thee be praise, honour, thanksgiving, and adoration, now, etc.

The Deacons approach, and he signs each one of them on the forehead, saying:

Christ accept thy ministry: Christ cause thy face to shine: Christ save thy life: Christ make thy youth to grow.

And they respond:

Christ accept thy oblation.

XVIII. *All return to their own place; and the Priest, after bowing, rises and says in the tone of the Gospel:*

The grace of our Lord Jesus Christ, and the love of God the Father, and the communion of the Holy Ghost, be with us all.

The Priest signs himself, and lifts up his hand over his head, so that it should be in the air, and the people be partakers in the signing:

The Deacon says:

We all with fear: *and at these words,* He hath given to us His mysteries.

The Priest begins to break the body, and says:

Be merciful, O Lord, through Thy clemency to the sins and follies of Thy servants, and sanctify our lips through

Thy grace, that they may give the fruits of glory and praise to Thy divinity, with all Thy saints in Thy kingdom.

And, raising his voice, he says:

And make us worthy, O Lord our God, to stand before Thee continually without stain, with pure heart, with open countenance, and with the confidence which is from Thee, mercifully granted to us: and let us all with one accord invoke Thee, and say thus: Our Father, etc.

The People say:

Our Father.

The Priest.

O Lord God Almighty, O Lord and our good God, who art full of mercy, we beg Thee, O Lord our God, and beseech the clemency of Thy goodness; lead us not into temptation, but deliver and save us from the evil one and his hosts; because Thine is the kingdom, the power, the strength, the might, and the dominion in heaven and on earth, now and always.

He signs himself, and they respond:

Amen.

XIX. *And he proceeds:*

Peace be with you.

They respond:

With thee and with thy spirit.

He proceeds:

It is becoming that the holy things should be to the holy in perfection.

And they say:

One holy Father: one holy Son: one Holy Ghost. Glory be to the Father, and to the Son, and to the Holy Ghost, for ever and ever. Amen.

The Deacon.

Praise ye.

And they say the responsory. And when the Deacon comes to carry the chalice, he says:

Let us pray for peace with us.

The Priest says:

The grace of the Holy Ghost be with thee, with us, and with those who receive Him.

And he gives the chalice to the Deacon. The Deacon says:

Bless, O Lord.

The Priest.

The gift of the grace of our Life-giver and Lord Jesus Christ be completed, in mercies, with all.

And he signs the people with the cross. In the meantime the responsories are said.

Brethren, receive the body of the Son, cries the church, and drink ye His chalice with faith in the house of His kingdom.

On feast-days.

Strengthen, O Lord.

On the Lord's day.

O Lord Jesus Christ.

Daily.

The mysteries which we have received.

The responsories being ended, the Deacon says:

All therefore.

And they respond:

Glory be to Himself on account of His ineffable gift.

LITURGY OF THE HOLY APOSTLES. 91

The Deacon.

Let us pray for peace with us.

The Priest at the middle of the altar says this prayer:

XX. It is meet, O Lord, just and right in all days, times, and hours, to thank, adore, and praise the awful name of Thy majesty, because Thou hast through Thy grace, O Lord, made us, mortal men possessing a frail nature, worthy to sanctify Thy name with the heavenly [1] beings, and to become partakers of the mysteries of Thy gift, and to be delighted with the sweetness of Thy oracles. And voices of glory and thanksgiving we ever offer up to Thy sublime divinity, O Lord.

Another.

Christ, our God, Lord, King, Saviour, and Life-giver, through His grace has made us worthy to receive His body and His precious and all-sanctifying blood. May He grant unto us that we may be pleasing unto Him in our words, works, thoughts, and deeds, so that that pledge which we have received may be to us for the pardon of our offences, the forgiveness of our sins, and the grand hope of a resurrection from the dead, and a new and true life in the kingdom of the heavens, with all who have been pleasing before Him, through His grace and His mercies for ever.

On ordinary days.

Praise, O Lord, honour, blessing, and thanksgiving we ought to ascribe to Thy glorious Trinity for the gift of Thy holy mysteries, which Thou hast given to us for the propitiation of our offences, O Lord of all.

Another.

Blessed be Thy adorable honour, from Thy glorious place, O Christ, the propitiator of our offences and our sins, and who takest away our follies through Thy renowned, holy,

[1] Spiritualibus.

life-giving, and divine mysteries. Christ the hope of our nature always and for ever. Amen.

Obsignation or final benediction.

May our Lord Jesus Christ, to whom we have ministered, and whom we have seen and honoured in His renowned, holy, life-giving, and divine mysteries, Himself render us worthy of the splendid glory of His kingdom, and of gladness with His holy angels, and for confidence before Him, that we may stand at His right hand. And on our entire congregation may His mercies and compassion be continually poured out, now and always, and ever.

On the Lord's day and on feast-days.

May He Himself who blessed us with all spiritual blessings in the heavens, through Jesus Christ our Lord, and prepared us for His kingdom, and called us to the desirable good things which neither cease nor perish, as He promised to us in His life-giving gospel, and said to the blessed congregation of His disciples: Verily, verily I say unto you, that every one who eateth my body and drinketh my blood, abideth in me, and I in him, and I will raise him up at the last day; and he cometh not to judgment, but I will make him pass from death to eternal life,—may He Himself now bless this congregation, and maintain our position, and render glorious our people who have come and rejoiced in receiving His renowned, holy, life-giving, and divine mysteries; and may ye be sealed and guarded by the holy sign of the Lord's cross from all evils, secret and open, now and always.

SYRIAC DOCUMENTS

OF

THE ANTE-NICENE PERIOD.

TRANSLATED BY

REV. B. P. PRATTEN, B.A.

INTRODUCTION TO AMBROSE AND MARA BAR SERAPION.

THE text of the two following short pieces is found in the *Spicilegium Syriacum* of the late Dr. Cureton. This careful scholar speaks of the second of these compositions as containing "some very obscure passages." The same remark holds good also of the first. Dr. Payne Smith describes them both as "full of difficulties." So far as these arise from errors in the text, they might have been removed, had I been able to avail myself of the opportunity kindly offered me by Dr. Rieu, Keeper of the Oriental MSS. at the British Museum, of inspecting the original MS. As it is, several have, it is hoped, been successfully met by conjecture.

To Dr. R. Payne Smith, Dean of Canterbury, who, as on two previous occasions, has most kindly and patiently afforded me his valuable assistance, I beg to offer my very grateful acknowledgments.

B. P. PRATTEN.

AMBROSE.[1]

MEMORIAL[2] which Ambrose, a chief man of Greece, wrote: who became a Christian, and all his fellow-senators raised an outcry against him; and he fled from them, and wrote and pointed out to them all their foolishness.

Beginning his discourse,[3] he answered and said:—

Think not, men of Greece, that my separation from your customs has been made without a just and proper reason. For I acquainted myself with all your wisdom, [consisting] of poetry, of oratory, of philosophy; and, when I found not [there] anything [agreeable to what is] right, or that is worthy of the Divine nature, I resolved to make myself acquainted with the wisdom of the Christians also, and to learn and see who [they are], and when [they took their rise], and what is [the nature of] this new and strange wisdom [of theirs],[4] or on what good [hopes] those who are imbued with it rely, that they speak [only] that which is true.

Men of Greece, when I came to examine [the Christian writings], I found not any folly[5] [in them], as I had found

---

[1] This piece has much in common with the *Discourse to the Greeks* (Λόγος πρὸς Ἕλληνας), ascribed by many to Justin, which is contained in vol. ii. pp. 279-283 of this *Library*. Two things seem to be evident: (1) That neither of the two pieces is the original composition: for each contains something not found in the other; (2) That the original was in Greek: for the Syriac has in some instances evidently mistranslated the Greek.

[2] The Greek ὑπομνήματα.

[3] Lit., "and in the beginning of his words."

[4] Lit., "what is the newness and strangeness of it."

[5] The word also means "sin;" and this notion is the more prominent of the two in what follows.

in the celebrated Homer, who has said concerning the wars of the two trials:[1] "Because of Helen, many of the Greeks perished at Troy, away from their beloved home."[2] For, first of all, we are told[3] concerning Agamemnon their king, that by reason of the foolishness of his brother Menelaus, and the violence of his madness, and the uncontrollable nature of his passion, he resolved to go and rescue Helen from [the hands of] a certain leprous[4] shepherd; and [afterwards], when the Greeks had become victorious in the war, and burnt cities, and taken women and children captive, and the land was filled with blood, and the rivers with corpses, Agamemnon himself also was found to be taken captive by [his] passion for Briseis. Patroclus, again, we are told, was slain, and Achilles, the son of the goddess Thetis, mourned over him; Hector was dragged [along the ground], and Priam and Hecuba together were weeping over the loss of their children; Astyanax, the son of Hector, was thrown down from the walls of Ilion, and his mother Andromache the mighty Ajax bore away [into captivity]; and that which was taken as booty was, after a little while, [all] squandered in sensual indulgence.

Of the wiles of Odysseus the son of Laertes, and of his murders, who shall tell the tale? For of a hundred and ten suitors did his house in one day become the grave, and

---

[1] It is difficult to assign any satisfactory meaning to the word ܢܣܘܩܐ‎, which appears, however, to be the reading of the MS., since Cureton endeavours to justify the rendering given. "Calamities," a sense the word will also bear, seems no easier of explanation. If we could assume the meaning to be "nations" (*nationes*), a word similar in sound to that found in the text, explaining it of *heathen* peoples, Gentiles (comp. Tertullian, *de Idol.* 22, "per deos nationum"), this might seem to meet the difficulty. But there is no trace in this composition of a *Latin* influence: if a foreign word *must* be used, we should rather have expected the Greek ἔθνη.

[2] *Il.* ii. 177 sq.   [3] Lit., "they say."

[4] It has been proposed to substitute in the Greek copy λιπαροῦ, "dainty," for λεπροῦ. But the Syriac confirms the MS. reading. The term is thought to be expressive of the contempt in which shepherds were held. See vol. ii. p. 279, note 1.

it was filled with corpses and blood. He, too, [it was] that by his wickedness gained the praises [of men], because through [his] pre-eminence in craft he escaped detection; he, too, [it was] who, you say, sailed upon the sea, and heard [not] the voice of the Sirens [only] because he stopped his ears with wax.[1]

The famous Achilles, again, the son of Peleus, who bounded across the river, and routed[2] the Trojans, and slew Hector, —this said hero of yours became the slave of Philoxena, and was overcome by an Amazon [as she lay] dead and stretched [upon her bier]; and he put off his armour, and arrayed himself in nuptial garments, and finally fell a sacrifice to love.

Thus much concerning [your] great *men*;[3] and thou, Homer, hadst deserved forgiveness, if thy silly story-telling had gone so far [only] as to prate about men, and not about the gods. As for what [he says] about the gods, I am ashamed even to speak of it: for the stories that have been invented about them are very wicked and shocking; passing strange,[4] too, and not to be believed; and, if the truth must be told,[5] fit only to be laughed at. For a person will [be compelled to] laugh when he meets with them, and will not believe them when he hears them. For [think of] gods who did not one of them observe the laws of rectitude, or of purity, or of modesty, but [were] adulterers, and spent their time in debauchery, and [yet] were not condemned to death, as they ought to have been!

---

[1] In the Greek this is adduced as an evidence of his weakness: "because he was unable to stop his ears by [his] self-control (φρονήσει)."

[2] ܥܪܩ, the reading of the text, which can only mean "fled," is manifestly incorrect. The Aphel of this verb, ܐܥܪܩ, "caused to flee," is suggested by Dr. Payne Smith, who also proposes ܥܩܪ, "exstirpavit."

[3] Or, "[your] heroes."

[4] This is not intended as a translation of ܡܙܕܟܝܢ, which is literally "conquered." Dr. Payne Smith thinks it just possible that there was in the Greek some derivative of ὑπερβάλλω = "to surpass belief," which the Syrian translator misunderstood.

[5] This is conjectured to be the meaning of what would be literally rendered, "*et id quod coactum est.*"

Why, the sovereign of the gods, the very "father of gods and men," not only, as ye say, was an adulterer (this was but a light thing), but even slew his own father, and was a pæderast. I will first of all speak of [his] adultery, though I blush [to do so]: for he appeared to Antiope as a satyr, and descended upon Danaë as a shower of gold, and became a bull for Europa, and a swan for Leda; whilst the love of Semele, the mother of Dionysus, exposed both his own ardency [of passion] and the jealousy of the chaste Hera. Ganymede the Phrygian, too, he carried off [disguised] as an eagle, that the fair and comely boy, forsooth, might serve as cup-bearer to him. This said sovereign of the gods, moreover, killed his father Kronos, that he might seize upon his kingdom.

Oh! to how many charges is the sovereign of the gods amenable,[1] and how many deaths does he deserve [to die], as an adulterer, and as a sorcerer,[2] and as a pæderast! Read to the sovereign of the gods, O men of Greece, the law concerning parricide, and the condemnation pronounced on adultery, and [about] the shame that attaches to the vile sin of pæderasty. How many adulterers has the sovereign of the gods indoctrinated [in sin]! Nay, how many pæderasts, and sorcerers, and murderers! So that, if a man be found indulging his passions, he must not be put to death: because he has done this that he may become like the sovereign of the gods; and, if he be found a murderer, he has an excuse [in] the sovereign of the gods; and, if a man be a sorcerer, he has learned it from the sovereign of the gods; and, if he be a pæderast, the sovereign of the gods is his apologist. Then, again, if one should speak of courage, Achilles was more valiant than this said sovereign of the gods: for he slew the man that slew his friend; but the sovereign of the gods wept over Sarpedon his son when he was dying, being distressed [for him].

Pluto, again, who is a god, carried off Kora,[3] and the

---

[1] Lit., "of how many censures is . . . full."

[2] Since he could change his form to suit his purpose.

[3] That is, "the Daughter" (namely, of Demeter), the name under which Proserpine was worshipped in Attica.

mother of Kora was hurrying hither and thither searching for her daughter in all desert places; and, [although] Alexander Paris, when he had carried off Helen, paid the penalty of vengeance, as [having made himself] her lover by force, yet Pluto, who is a god, when he carried off Kora, remained without rebuke; and, [although] Menelaus, who is a man, knew how to search for Helen his wife, yet Demeter, who is a goddess, knew not where to search for Kora her daughter.

Let Hephæstus put away jealousy from him, and not indulge resentment.[1] For he was hated,[2] because he was old and lame; while Ares was loved, because he was a youth and beautiful in form. There was, however, a reproof [administered in respect] of the adultery. Hephæstus was not, indeed, [at first] aware of the love existing between Venus[3] his wife and Ares; but, when he did become acquainted with it, Hephæstus said: "Come, see a ridiculous and senseless piece of behaviour—how to me, who am her own, Venus, the daughter of the sovereign of the gods, is offering insult—to me, [I say] who am her own, and is paying honour to Ares, who is a stranger to her." But to the sovereign of the gods it was not displeasing: for he loved such as were like these. Penelope, moreover, remained a widow twenty years, because she was expecting [the return of] her husband Odysseus, and busied herself with cunning tasks,[4] and persevered in works of skill, while all those suitors kept pressing her [to marry them]; but Venus, who is a goddess, when Hephæstus her husband was close to her, deserted him, because she was overcome by love for Ares. Hearken, men of Greece: which of you would have dared to do this, or would even have endured to see it? And, if any one *should* dare [to

---

[1] Because the behaviour of which he had to complain was sanctioned by the highest of the gods.

[2] For ܐܬܢܣܝ, "was tried," read ܐܬܢܣܝ. The Greek has μεμίσητο. Cureton: "forgotten."

[3] The word is "Balthi."

[4] Dr. Payne Smith reads ܡܟܝܢܬܐ instead of ܡܟܝܠܬܐ, a word which, as Cureton says, is not in the lexicons.

act so], what torture would be in store for him, or what scourgings!

Kronos, again, who is a god, who devoured all those children [of his], was not even brought before a court of justice. They further tell [us] that the sovereign of the gods, his son, was the only one that escaped from him; and that the madness of Kronos his father was cheated [of its purpose] because Rhea his wife, the mother of the sovereign of the gods, offered him a stone in the place of the said sovereign of the gods, his son, to prevent him from devouring him. Hearken, men of Greece, and reflect upon this madness! Why, [even] the dumb animal that grazes in the field knows its [proper] food, and does not touch strange food; the wild beast, too, and the reptile, and the bird, know their food. As for men, I need not say anything about them: ye yourselves are acquainted with their food, and understand it [well]. But Kronos, who is a god, not knowing his [proper] food, ate up a stone!

Therefore, O men of Greece, if ye will have such gods as these, do not find fault with one another when ye do such-like things. Be not angry with thy son when he forms the design to kill thee: because he [thus] resembles the sovereign of the gods. And, if a man commit adultery with thy wife, why dost thou think of him as an enemy, and yet to the sovereign of the gods, who is like him, doest worship and service? Why, too, dost thou find fault with thy wife when she has committed adultery and leads a dissolute life,[1] and [yet] payest honour to Venus, and placest her [images] in shrines? Persuade [your] Solon to repeal his laws; Lycurgus, also, to make no laws; let the Areopagus repeal[2] theirs, and judge no more; and let the Athenians have councils no longer. Let the Athenians discharge Socrates [from his office]: for no one like Kronos has [ever] come before him. Let them not put to death Orestes, who killed his mother: for, lo!

---

[1] The reading of the Greek copy, ἀκολάστως ζῶσαν, is here given. The Syrian adapter, misunderstanding ἀκολάστως, renders: "and is without punishment."

[2] Cureton, "break."

the sovereign of the gods did worse things than these to his father. Œdipus also [too] hastily inflicted mischief on himself, in depriving his eyes of sight, because he had killed his mother unwittingly: for he did not think about[1] the sovereign of the gods, who killed his father and [yet] remained without punishment. Medea, again, who killed her children, the Corinthians banish [from their country]; and [yet] they do service and honour to Kronos, who devoured his children. Then, too, as regards Alexander Paris—he was right in carrying off Helen: [for he did it] that he might become like Pluto, who carried off Kora. Let [your] men be set free from law, and let [your] cities be [the abode] of wanton women, and a dwelling-place for sorcerers.

Wherefore, O men of Greece, seeing that your gods are grovelling like yourselves, and your heroes destitute of courage,[2] as your dramas tell and your stories declare—then, again, [what shall be said] of the tribulations of Orestes; and the couch of Thyestes; and the foul taint [in the family] of Pelops; and concerning Danaus, who through jealousy killed his sons [-in-law], and deprived them of offspring; the banquet of Thyestes, too, [feeding upon] the corpse [set before him by way] of vengeance for her [whom he had wronged]; [about] Procne also, to this hour screaming as she flies; her sister too, warbling with her tongue cut out?[3] What, moreover, is it fitting to say about the murder committed by Œdipus, who took his own mother [to wife], and whose brothers killed one another, they being [at the same time] his sons?

Your festivals, too, I hate; for there is no moderation where they are; the sweet flutes also, dispellers of care, which play as an incitement to dancing;[4] and the preparation of oint-

[1] Lit., "look at."
[2] So in the Greek copy. The Syriac, which has "valiant," appears to have mistaken ἀνάνδροι for ἀνδρεῖοι.
[3] The tradition seems to be followed which makes Procne to have been changed into a swallow, and her sister (Philomela) into a nightingale.
[4] Cureton: "play with a tremulous motion." But the Syriac very well answers to the Greek ἐκκαλούμενοι πρὸς οἰστρώδεις κινήσεις, if we take ܠ to denote *result:* q.d., "so as to produce [movement]."

ments, wherewith ye anoint yourselves; and the chaplets which ye put on. In the abundance of your wickedness, too, ye have forgotten shame, and your understandings have become blinded, and ye have been infuriated[1] by the heat [of passion], and have loved the adulterous bed.[2]

Had these things been said by another, perhaps [our adversaries] would have brought an accusation against him, [on the plea] that they were untrue. But your own poets say them, and your own hymns and dramas declare them.

Come, therefore, and be instructed in the word of God, and in the wisdom which is fraught with comfort. Rejoice, and become partakers of it. Acquaint yourselves with the King Immortal, and acknowledge His servants. For not in arms do they make their boast, nor do they commit murders: because our Commander has no delight in abundance of strength, nor yet in horsemen and their gallant array, nor yet in illustrious descent; but He delights in the pure soul, fenced round by a rampart of righteousness. The word of God, moreover, and the promises of our good King, and the works of God, are ever teaching us. Oh [the blessedness of] the soul that is redeemed by the power of the word! Oh [the blessedness of] the trumpet of peace without war! Oh [the blessedness of] the teaching which quenches the fire of appetite! which, [though it] makes not poets, nor fits [men] to be philosophers, nor has [among its votaries] the orators of the crowd; yet instructs [men], and makes the dead not to die, and lifts men from the earth [as] gods up to the region which is above the firmament. Come, be instructed, and be like me: for I too was [once] as ye are.

[1] Greek, ἐκβακχευόμενοι.   [2] Lit., "bed of falsity."

A LETTER OF MARA, SON OF SERAPION.

MARA, son of Serapion, to Serapion, my son: peace.

When thy master and guardian wrote me a letter, and informed me that thou wast very diligent in study, [though so] young in years, I blessed God that thou, a little boy, [and] without a guide [to direct thee], hadst begun in good earnest; and to myself [also] this was a comfort—that I heard of thee, little boy [as thou art, as displaying] such greatness of mind and conscientiousness:[1] [a character] which, in the case of many [who have begun well], has shown no eagerness to continue.

On this account, lo, I have written for thee this record, [touching] that which I have by careful observation discovered in the world. For the kind of life men lead has been carefully observed by me. I tread the path of learning,[2] and from the study of Greek philosophy[3] have I found out all these things, although they suffered shipwreck when the birth of life took place.[4]

---

[1] Lit., "good conscience."

[2] Or, "my daily converse is with learning." So Dr. Payne Smith is inclined to take these difficult words, supplying, as Cureton evidently does, the pronoun ܐܢܐ. The construction would be easier if we could take the participle ܡܬܗܠܟ as a passive, and render: "It (the kind of life men lead) has been *explored* by me by means of study."

[3] Lit., "Græcism."

[4] The meaning probably is, that the maxims referred to lost their importance for him when he entered upon the new life of a Christian (so Cureton), or their importance to mankind when Christianity itself was born into the world. But why he did not substitute more distinctive Christian teaching is not clear. Perhaps the fear of persecution influenced him.

Be diligent, then, my son, in [attention to] those things which are becoming for the free,[1] [so as] to devote thyself to learning, and to follow after wisdom; and endeavour thus to become confirmed in those [habits] with which thou hast begun. Call to mind also my precepts, as a quiet person who is fond of the pursuit of learning. And, even though [such a life] should seem to thee very irksome, [yet] when thou hast made experience of it for a little while, it will become very pleasant to thee: for to me also it so happened. When, moreover, a person has left his home, and is able [still] to preserve his [previous] character, and properly does that which it behoves him to do, he is that chosen man who is called "the blessing of God," and one who does not find aught else to compare with his freedom.[2] For, as for those persons who are called to the pursuit of learning, they are seeking to extricate themselves from the turmoils of time; and those who take hold upon wisdom, they are clinging to the hope of righteousness; and those who take their stand on truth, they are displaying the banner of their virtue; and those who cultivate philosophy, they are looking to escape from the vexations of the world. And do thou too, my son, thus wisely behave thyself in [regard to] these things, as a wise person who seeks to spend a pure life; and [beware] lest the gain which many hunger after enervate thee, and thy mind turn to covet riches, which have no stability. For, when they are acquired by fraud, they do not continue; nor, even when justly [obtained], do they last; and all those things which are seen by thee in the world, as belonging to that which is [only] for a little time, [are destined] to depart like a dream: for they are [but as] the risings and settings of the seasons.

About the [objects of that] vainglory, too, of which the life of men is full, be not thou solicitous: seeing that from those things which give us joy there quickly comes to us harm. Most especially [is this the case with] the birth of

---

[1] That is, the matters constituting "a *liberal* education."

[2] Cureton's less literal rendering probably gives the true sense: "with whose liberty nothing else can be compared."

beloved children. For in two respects it plainly brings us harm: in the case of the virtuous, [our very] affection for them torments us, and from their [very excellence of] character we suffer torture; and, in the case of the vicious, we are worried with their correction, and afflicted with their misconduct.

Thou hast heard,[1] moreover, concerning our companions, that, when they were leaving Samosata, they were distressed [about it], and, as if complaining of the time [in which their lot was cast], said thus: "We are now far removed from our home, and we cannot return [again] to our city, or behold our people, or offer to our gods the greeting of praise." Meet was it that that day should be called [a day] of lamentation, because one heavy grief possessed them all alike. For they wept as they remembered their fathers, and [they thought of] their mothers[2] with sobs, and they were distressed for their brethren, [and] grieved for their betrothed whom they had left behind. And, although we had heard that their[3] former companions were proceeding to Seleucia, we clandestinely [set out, and] proceeded on the way towards them, and united our own misery with theirs. Then was our grief exceedingly violent, and fitly did our weeping abound, by reason of our desperate plight, and our wailing gathered [itself into] a dense cloud,[4] and our misery grew vaster than a mountain: for not one of us had the power to ward off the disasters that assailed him. For affection for the living was intense, as well as sorrow for the dead, and our miseries were driving us on without any way [of escape]. For we saw our brethren and our children captives, and we remembered our deceased companions, who were laid [to rest] in a foreign[5] land. Each one of us, too, was anxious

---

[1] Cureton: "I have heard." The unpointed text is here ambiguous.

[2] Read ܐܘܡܗܬܢ, instead of ܐܘܡܘܬܢ, "peoples."

[3] Perhaps "our" is meant.

[4] Cureton: "and the dark cloud collected our sighs." But the words immediately following, as well as the fact that in each of the clauses the nominative is placed last, favours the rendering given.

[5] Lit., "borrowed."

for himself, lest he should have disaster added to disaster, or [lest] another calamity should overtake that which went before it. What enjoyment could men have that were prisoners, [and] who experienced [things like] these?

But as for thee, my beloved, be not distressed because in thy loneliness thou hast[1] been driven from place to place. For to these things men are born, since they [are destined] to meet with the accidents of time. But [rather] let thy thought be this, that to wise men every place is alike, and [that] in every city the good have many fathers and mothers. Else, [if thou doubt it], take thee a proof from [what thou hast seen] thyself. How many people who know thee not love thee as [one of] their own children; and [what] a host of women receive thee as [they would] their own beloved ones! Verily, as a stranger thou hast been fortunate; verily, for thy small love many people have conceived an ardent affection for thee.

What, again, are we to say concerning the delusion[2] which has taken up its abode in the world? Both by reason of toil[3] painful is the journey through it, and by its agitations are we, like a reed by the force of the wind, bent now in this direction, now in that. For I have been amazed at many who cast away their children, and I have been astonished at others who bring up those that are not theirs. There are persons who acquire riches in the world, and I have also been astonished at others who inherit that which is not [of] their own [acquisition]. Thus [mayest thou] understand and see that we are walking under the guidance of delusion.

Begin and tell us, O wisest of men,[4] on which of [his] possessions a man can place reliance, or concerning what things he can say that they are such as abide. [Wilt thou

---

[1] Lit., "because thy loneliness has."

[2] Or "error." He may refer either to the delusion of those who pursue supposed earthly good, or to the false appearances by which men are deceived in such pursuit.

[3] For ܒܥܡܠܐ read ܥܡܠܐ.

[4] Cureton: "A sage among men once began to say to us." This would require ܫܪܝ, not ܫܪܐ.

say so] of abundance of riches? they are snatched away. Of fortresses? they are spoiled. Of cities? they are laid waste. Of greatness? it is brought down. Of magnificence? it is overthrown. Of beauty? it withers. Or of laws? they pass away. Or of poverty? it is despised. Or of children? they die. Or of friends? they prove false. Or of the praises [of men]? jealousy goes before them.

Let a man, therefore, rejoice in his empire, like Darius; or in his good fortune, like Polycrates; or in his bravery, like Achilles; or in his wife, like Agamemnon; or in his offspring, like Priam; or in his skill, like Archimedes; or in his wisdom, like Socrates; or in his learning, like Pythagoras; or in his ingenuity, like Palamedes;—the life of men, my son, departs from the world, but their praises and their virtues abide for ever.

Do thou, then, my little son, choose thee that which fadeth not away. For those who occupy themselves with these things are called modest, and [are] beloved, and lovers of a good name.

When, moreover, anything untoward befalls thee, do not lay the blame on man, nor be angry against God, nor fulminate against the time thou livest in.

If thou shalt continue in this mind, thy gift is not small which thou hast received from God, which has no need of riches, and is never reduced to poverty. For without fear shalt thou pass thy life,[1] and with rejoicing. For fear and apologies for [one's] nature belong not to the wise, but to such as walk contrary to law. For no man has ever been deprived of his wisdom, as of his property.

Follow diligently learning rather than riches. For the greater are [one's] possessions, the greater is the evil [attendant upon them]. For I have myself observed that, where [a man's] goods are many, so also are the tribulations which happen [to him]; and, where luxuries are accumulated, there also do sorrows congregate; and, where riches are abundant, there is [stored up] the bitterness of many a year.

If, therefore, thou shalt behave with understanding, and

---

[1] ܚܠܨܒܪ.

shalt diligently watch over [thy conduct], God will not refrain from helping thee, nor men from loving thee.

Let that which thou art able to acquire suffice thee; and if, moreover, thou art able to do without property, thou shalt be called blessed, and no man whatsoever shall be jealous of thee.

And remember also this, that nothing will disturb thy life very greatly, except [it be the love of] gain; [and] that no man after his death is called an owner of property: because it is by the desire of this that weak men are led captive, and they know not that a man dwells among his possessions [only] in the manner of a chance-comer, and they are haunted with fear because these [possessions] are not secured to them: for they have abandoned that which is their own, and seek that which is not theirs.

What are we to say, when the wise are dragged by force by the hands of tyrants, and their wisdom is deprived of its freedom[1] by slander, and they are plundered for their [superior] intelligence, without [the opportunity of making] a defence? [They are not wholly to be pitied.] For what benefit did the Athenians obtain by putting Socrates to death, seeing that they received [as] retribution for it famine and pestilence? Or the people of Samos by the burning of Pythagoras, seeing that in one hour the whole[2] of their country was covered with sand? Or the Jews [by the murder] of their Wise King, seeing that from that very time their kingdom was driven away [from them]? For with justice did God grant a recompense to the wisdom of [all] three of them. For the Athenians died by famine; and the people of Samos were covered by the sea without remedy; and the Jews, brought to desolation and expelled from their kingdom, are driven away into every land. [Nay], Socrates did *not* die, because of Plato; nor yet Pythagoras, because of the statue of Hera; nor yet the Wise King, because of the new laws which he enacted.

Moreover I, my son, have attentively observed mankind,

---

[1] Lit., "made captive."
[2] For ܗܟܠܗ read ܟܠܗ.

[and noticed] in what a dismal state of ruin they are. And I have been amazed that they are not utterly prostrated[1] by the calamities which surround them, and [that] even [their] wars[2] are not enough for them, nor the pains [they endure], nor the diseases, nor the death, nor the poverty; but [that], like savage beasts, they must needs rush upon one another in [their] enmity, [trying] which of them shall inflict the greater mischief on his fellow. For they have broken away from the bounds of truth, and transgress all honest laws, because they are bent on fulfilling their selfish desires (for, whensoever a man is eagerly set on [obtaining] that which he desires, how is it possible that he should fitly do that which it behoves him [to do]?); and they acknowledge no restraint,[3] and but seldom stretch out their hands towards truth and goodness, but in their manner of life behave like the deaf[4] and the blind. Moreover, the wicked rejoice, and the righteous are disquieted. He that has, denies [that he has]; and he that has not, struggles to acquire. The poor seek [help], and the rich hide [their wealth], and every man laughs at his fellow. Those that are drunken are stupefied, and those that have recovered themselves are ashamed.[5] Some weep, and some sing; and some laugh, and others are a prey to care. They rejoice in things evil, and a man that speaks the truth they despise.

Should a man, then, be surprised when the world is seeking to wither him with [its] scorn, seeing that they [and he] have not one [and the same] manner of life? *These* are the things for which they care. One of them is looking [forward to the time] when in battle he shall obtain the renown of victory; yet the valiant perceive not by how many foolish objects of desire a man is led captive in the world. But would that for a little while self-repentance visited them!

---

[1] No verb is found in the lexicons to which ܐܠܨܩܐܘ can be referred. It may perhaps be Eshtaphel of a verb ܟܦܐ, cognate with ܟܦ, "to be bent."

[2] For ܩܪܒܘ read ܩܪܒܐ. [3] Or "moderation."
[4] Cureton: "dumb." The word ܚܪܫܐ has both senses.
[5] Or "penitent."

For, while victorious by their bravery, they are overcome by the power of covetousness. For I have made trial of men, and with this result: that the one thing on which they are intent, is abundance of riches. Therefore also it is that they have no settled purpose; but, through the instability of their minds, a man is of a sudden cast down [from his elation of spirit] to be swallowed up with sadness. They look not at the vast wealth of eternity, [nor consider] that every visitation of trouble is conducting us all alike to the same [final] period. For they are devoted to the majesty of the belly, [that] huge blot [on the character] of the vicious.

Moreover, [as regards] this [letter] which it has come into my mind to write to thee, it is not enough to read it, but the best thing is that it be put in practice.[1] For I know for myself, that when thou shalt have made experiment of this mode of life, it will be very pleasant to thee, and thou wilt be free from sore vexation; because it is [only] on account of children that we tolerate riches.[2]

Put, therefore, sadness away from thee, O [most] beloved of mankind,—a thing which never in anywise benefits [a man]; and drive care away from thee, which brings with it no advantage whatsoever. For we have no resource or skill [that can avail us—nothing] but a great mind [able] to cope with the disasters and to endure the tribulations which we are always receiving at the hands of the times. For at these things does it behove us to look, and not [only] at those which are fraught with rejoicing and good repute.

Devote thyself to wisdom, the fount of all things good, the treasure that faileth not. There shalt thou lay thy head, and be at ease. For this shall be to thee father and mother, and a good companion for thy life.

---

[1] So Dr. Payne Smith, who is inclined to take ܟܠ ܡܠܝ ܒܗ in the sense, "it goes before, it is best, with respect to it." Cureton translates, "it should also proceed to practice," joining ܢܗܘܐ with the participle just mentioned; whereas Dr. Smith connects it with ܕܣܥܪ܂, thus: "but that it should be [put] in practice is best with respect to it."

[2] This appears to show that the life of learned seclusion which he has been recommending is one of celibacy—monasticism.

A LETTER OF MARA.

Enter into closest intimacy with fortitude and patience, those [virtues] which are able [successfully] to encounter the tribulations that befall feeble men. For so great is their strength, that they are adequate to sustain hunger, and [can] endure thirst, and mitigate every trouble. With toil, moreover, yea even with dissolution, they make right merry.

To these things give diligent attention, and thou shalt lead an untroubled life, and I also shall have comfort,[1] and thou shalt be called "the delight of his parents."

For in that time of yore, when our city was standing in her greatness, thou mayest be aware that against many persons [among us] abominable words were uttered; but for ourselves,[2] we acknowledged long ago that we received love, no less than honour, to the fullest extent from the multitude of her people: it was the state of the times [only] that forbade [our] completing those things which we had resolved on doing.[3] And here also in the prison-house we give thanks to God that we have received the love of many: for we are striving to our utmost to maintain a life of sobriety and cheerfulness;[4] and, if any one drive us by force, he will [but] be bearing public testimony against himself, that he is estranged from all things good, and he will receive disgrace and shame from the foul mark of shame [that is upon him]. For we have shown our truth—[that truth] which in our [now] ruined kingdom we possessed not.[5] But, if the

---

[1] Or, "and thou shalt be to me a comfort," as Cureton.

[2] That is, "myself."

[3] Such appears to be the sense of this obscure passage. The literal rendering is, "We acknowledged of old that we received equal love and honour to the fullest extent from her multitude" (or, from her greatness); "but the time forbade [our] completing those things which were [already] accomplished in our mind." What things he refers to (for his words seem to have a particular reference) is not clear. The word rendered "greatness," or "multitude," is in reality two words in pointed MSS. Here it does not appear, except from the sense, which is intended.

[4] Lit., "We are putting ourself to the proof to [see how far we can] stand in wisdom," etc.

[5] "This is a very hopeless passage. . . . Perhaps the codex has ܣܘܪܒܢ, 'the kingdom of *our* ruin,' *i.e.* the ruined country in which

Romans shall permit us to go [back] to our own country, [as called upon] by justice and righteousness [to do], they will be acting like humane men, and will earn the name of good and righteous, and at the same time [will have] a peaceful country in which to dwell: for they will exhibit their greatness when they shall leave us free men, [and] we shall be obedient to the sovereign power which the time has allotted to us. But let them not, like tyrants, drive us as [though we were] slaves. Yet, if it has been [already] determined what shall be done, we shall receive nothing more [dreadful] than the peaceful death which is in store for us.

But thou, my little son, if thou resolve diligently to acquaint thyself with these things, first of all put a check on appetite, and set limits to that in which thou art [indulging]. Seek the power to refrain from being angry; and, instead of [yielding to] outbursts of passion, listen to [the promptings of] kindness.

For myself, what I am henceforth solicitous about is this —[that], so far as I have recollections [of the past], I may leave behind me a book [containing them], and with a prudent mind finish the journey which I am appointed [to take], and depart without suffering out of the sad afflictions of the world. For my prayer is, that I may receive [my] dismissal; and [by] what kind of death concerns me not. But, if any one should be troubled or anxious [about this], I have no counsel to give him: for yonder, in the dwelling-place of all the world, will he find us before him.

One of his friends asked Mara, son of Serapion, when in bonds at his side: "Nay, by thy life, Mara, tell me what [cause] of laughter thou hast seen, that thou laughest." "I am laughing," said Mara, "at Time:[1] inasmuch as, although he has not borrowed any evil from me, he is paying me back."

[Here] ends the letter of Mara, son of Serapion.

we used to dwell. For possibly it refers to what he has said before about the ruined greatness of his city, captured by the Romans. I suppose Mara was a Persian."—DR. PAYNE SMITH.

[1] Or, "the time."

SELECTIONS FROM THE PROPHETIC SCRIPTURES.

TRANSLATED BY

REV. WILLIAM WILSON, M.A.

SELECTIONS FROM THE PROPHETIC SCRIPTURES.

I. THOSE around Sedrach, Misak, and Abednago in the furnace of fire, say as they praise God, "Bless, ye heavens, the Lord; praise and exalt Him for ever;" then, "Bless, ye angels, the Lord;" then, "Bless the Lord, all ye waters that are above heaven." So the Scriptures assign the heavens and the waters to the class of pure powers [spirits], as is shown in Genesis. Suitably, then, inasmuch as "power" is used with a variety of meaning, Daniel adds, "Let every power bless the Lord;" then, further, "Bless the Lord, sun and moon;" and, "Bless the Lord, ye stars of heaven. Bless the Lord, all ye that worship [Him]; praise and confess the God of gods, for His mercy is for ever." It is written in Daniel, on the occasion of the three children praising in the furnace.

II. "Blessed art Thou, who lookest on the abysses as Thou sittest on the cherubim," says Daniel, in agreement with Enoch, who said, "And I saw all sorts of matter." For the abyss, which is in its essence boundless, is bounded by the power of God. These material essences then, from which the separate genera and their species are produced, are called abysses; since you would not call the water alone the abyss, although matter is allegorically called water, the abyss.

III. "In the beginning God made the heaven and the earth" (Gen. i. 1), both terrestrial and celestial things. And that this is true, the Lord said to Osee, "Go, take to thyself a wife of fornication, and children of fornication: because the land committing fornication, shall commit fornication, [departing] from the Lord" (Hos. i. 2). For it is not the element [of earth] that he speaks of, but those that dwell in the element, those who have an earthly disposition.

IV. And that the Son is the beginning[1] [or head], Hosea teaches clearly: "And it shall be, that in the place in which it was said to them, Ye are not my people, they shall be called the children of the living God: and the children of Judah and the children of Israel shall be gathered to the same place, and they shall place over them one head,[2] and they shall come up out of the land ; for great is the day of Jezreel" (Hos. i. 10, 11). For whom one believes, him He chooses. But one believes the Son, who is the head; wherefore also he said in addition: "But I will have mercy on the sons of Judah, and will save them by the Lord their God" (Hos. i. 7). Now the Saviour who saves is the Son of God. He is then the head.[3]

V. The Spirit by Osee says, "I am your Instructor" (Hos. v. 2); "Blow ye[4] the trumpet upon the hills of the Lord; sound upon the high places" (Hos. v. 8). And is not baptism itself, which is the sign of regeneration, an escape from matter, by the teaching of the Saviour, a great impetuous stream, ever rushing on and bearing us along? The Lord accordingly, leading us out of disorder, illumines us by bringing us into the light, which is shadowless and is material no longer.

VI. This river and sea of matter two prophets[5] cut asunder and divided by the power of the Lord, the matter being bounded, through both divisions of the water. Famous leaders both, by whom the signs were believed, they complied with the will of God, so that the righteous man may proceed from matter, having journeyed through it first. On the one of these commanders also was imposed the name of our Saviour.[6]

VII. Now, regeneration is by water and spirit, as was all creation: "For the Spirit of God moved on the abyss"

---

[1] ἀρχή. [2] ἀρχήν. [3] ἀρχή.
[4] "Blow ye the cornet in Gibeah, and the trumpet in Ramah."—A. V.
[5] Moses who divided the sea, and Joshua who divided the Jordan.
[6] Joshua—Jesus.

(Gen. i. 2). And for this reason the Saviour was baptized, though not Himself needing to be so, in order that He might consecrate the whole water for those who were being regenerated. Thus it is not the body only, but the soul, that we cleanse. It is accordingly a sign of the sanctifying of our invisible part, and of the straining off from the new and spiritual creation of the unclean spirits that have got mixed up with the soul.

VIII. "The water above the heaven." Since baptism is performed by water and the Spirit as a protection against the twofold fire,—that which lays hold of what is visible, and that which lays hold of what is invisible; and of necessity, there being an immaterial element of water and a material, is it a protection against the twofold [1] fire. And the earthly water cleanses the body; but the heavenly water, by reason of its being immaterial and invisible, is an emblem of the Holy Spirit, who is the purifier of what is invisible, as the water of the Spirit, as the other of the body.

IX. God, out of goodness, hath mingled fear with goodness. For what is beneficial for each one, that He also supplies, as a physician to a sick man, as a father to his insubordinate child: "For he that spareth his rod hateth his son" (Prov. xiii. 24). And the Lord and His apostles walked in the midst of fear and labours. When, then, the affliction is sent in the person of a righteous man,[2] it is either from the Lord rebuking him for a sin committed before, or guarding him on account of the future, or not preventing by the exercise of His power an assault from without,[3]—for some good end to him and to those near, for the sake of example.

X. Now those that dwell in a corrupt body, like those who sail in an old ship, do not lie on their back, but are ever praying, stretching their hands to God.

XI. The ancients were exceedingly distressed, unless they had always some suffering in the body. For they were

---

[1] διπλόης—substantive. [2] ὅταν οὖν πιστοῦ σώματος ᾖ.

[3] The sense is hazy, but about as clear as that to be obtained by substituting conjecturally for προσβολήν (assault), πρὸς βολήν, or ἐπιβολήν, or ἐπιβουλήν.

afraid, that if they received not in this world the punishment of the sins which, in numbers through ignorance, accompany those that are in the flesh, they would in the other world suffer the penalty all at once. So that they preferred curative treatment here. What is to be dreaded is, then, not external disease, but sins, for which disease [comes], and disease of the soul, not of the body: "For all flesh is grass" (Isa. xl. 6), and corporeal and external good things are temporary; "but the things which are unseen are eternal" (2 Cor. iv. 18).

XII. As to knowledge, some elements of it we already possess; others, by what we do possess, we firmly hope [to attain]. For neither have we attained all, nor do we lack all. But we have received, as it were, an earnest of the eternal blessings, and of the ancestral riches. The provisions for the Lord's way are the Lord's beatitudes. For He said: "Seek," and anxiously seek, "the kingdom of God, and all these things shall be added to you: for the Father knoweth what things ye have need of" (Matt. vi. 33, 32). Thus He limits not only our occupations, but our cares. For He says: "Ye cannot, by taking thought, add aught to your stature" (Matt. vi. 27; Luke xii. 25). For God knows well what it is good for us to have and what to want. He wishes, therefore, that we, emptying ourselves of worldly cares, should be filled with that which is directed towards God. "For we groan, desiring to be clothed upon with that which is incorruptible, before putting off corruption." For when faith is shed abroad, unbelief is nonplussed. Similarly also with knowledge and righteousness. We must therefore not only empty the soul, but fill it with God. For no longer is there evil in it, since that has been made to cease; nor yet is there good, since it has not yet received good. But what is neither good nor evil is nothing. "For to the swept and empty house return" (Matt. xii. 44), if none of the blessings of salvation has been put in, the unclean spirit that dwelt there before, taking with him seven other unclean spirits. Wherefore, after emptying the soul of what is evil, we must fill with the good God that which is His chosen dwelling-place. For when the empty rooms are filled, then follows the seal, that the sanctuary may be guarded for God.

XIII. "By two and three witnesses every word is established" (Deut. xvii. 6). By Father, and Son, and Holy Spirit, by whose witness and help the prescribed commandments ought to be kept.

XIV. Fasting, according to the signification of the word, is abstinence from food. Now food makes us neither more righteous nor less. But mystically it shows that, as life is maintained in individuals by sustenance, and want of sustenance is the token of death; so also ought we to fast from worldly things, that we may die to the world, and after that, by partaking of divine sustenance, live to God. Especially does fasting empty the soul of matter, and make it, along with the body, pure and light for the divine words. Worldly food is, then, the former life and sins; but the divine food is faith, hope, love, patience, knowledge, peace, temperance. For "blessed are they that hunger and thirst after" God's "righteousness; for they shall be filled" (Matt. v. 6). The soul, but not the body, it is which is susceptible of this craving.

XV. The Saviour showed to the believing apostles prayer to be stronger than faith in the case of a demoniac, whom they could not cleanse, when He said, Such things are accomplished by prayer. He who has believed has obtained forgiveness of sins from the Lord; but he who has attained knowledge, inasmuch as he no longer sins, obtains from himself the forgiveness of the rest.

XVI. For as cures, and prophecies, and signs are performed by the agency of men, God working in them, so also is Gnostic teaching. For God shows His power through men. And the prophecy rightly says, "I will send to them a man who will save them" (Isa. xix. 20). Accordingly He sends forth at one time prophets, at another apostles, to be saviours of men. Thus God does good by the agency of men. For it is not that God can do some things, and cannot do others: He is never powerless in anything. No more are some things done with, and some things against His will; and some things by Him, and some things by another. But He even brought us into being by means of men, and trained us by means of men.

XVII. God made us, having previously no existence. For if we had a previous existence, we must have known where we were, and how and why we came hither. But if we had no pre-existence, then God is the sole author of our creation. As, then, He made us who had no existence, so also, now that we are made, He saves us by His own grace, if we show ourselves worthy and susceptible; if not, He[1] will let us pass to our proper end. For He is Lord both of the living and the dead.

XVIII. But see the power of God, not only in the case of men, in bringing to existence out of non-existence, and making them when brought into being grow up according to the progress of the time of life, but also in saving those who believe, in a way suitable to each individual. And now He changes both hours, and times, and fruits, and elements. For this is the one God, who has measured both the beginning and the end of events suitably to each one.

XIX. Advancing from faith and fear to knowledge, man knows how to say Lord, Lord; but not as His slave, he has learned to say, Our Father. Having set free the spirit of bondage, which produces fear, and advanced by love to adoption, he now reverences from love Him whom he feared before. For he no longer abstains from what he ought to abstain from out of fear, but out of love clings to the commandments. "The Spirit itself," it is said, "beareth witness when we cry, Abba, Father" (Rom. viii. 15; Gal. iv. 6).

XX. Now the Lord with His precious blood redeems us, freeing us from our old bitter masters, that is, our sins, on account of which the spiritual [powers] of wickedness ruled over us. Accordingly He leads us into the liberty of the Father,—sons that are co-heirs and friends. "For," says the Lord, "they that do the will of my Father are my brethren

---

[1] The reading is, $εἰ\ μὴ\ παρήσει\ πρὸς\ τὸ\ οἰκεῖον\ τέλος$; and the Latin translator renders, "si non segnes simus ad finem proprium." It seems better, with Sylburgius, to take $εἰ\ μὴ$ as equivalent to $εἰ\ δὲ\ μή$, and to put a comma after $μή$, so as to render as above.

and fellow-heirs" (Matt. xii. 50). "Call no man, therefore, father to yourselves on earth" (Matt. xxiii. 9). For it is masters that are on earth. But in heaven is the Father, of whom is the whole family, both in heaven and on earth (Eph. iii. 15). For love rules willing [hearts], but fear the unwilling. One kind of fear is base; but the other, leading us as a pedagogue to good, brings us to Christ, and is saving.

XXI. Now if one has a conception of God, it by no means corresponds with His worthiness. For what can the worthiness of God be? But let him, as far as is possible, conceive of a great and incomprehensible and most beautiful light; inaccessible, comprehending all good power, all comely virtue; caring for all, compassionate, passionless, good; knowing all things, foreknowing all things, pure, sweet, shining, stainless.

XXII. Since the movement of the soul is self-originated, the grace of God demands from it what the soul possesses, willingness as its contribution to salvation. For the soul wishes to be its own good; which the Lord, [however], gives it. For it is not devoid of sensation so as to be carried along like a body. Having is the result of taking, and taking of willing and desiring; and keeping hold of what one has received, of the exercise of care and of ability. Wherefore God has endowed the soul with free choice, that He may show it its duty, and that it choosing, may receive and retain.

XXIII. As through the body the Lord spake and healed, so also formerly by the prophets, and now by the apostles and teachers. For the church is the minister of the Lord's power. Thence He then assumed humanity,[1] that by it He might minister to the Father's will. And at all times, the God who loves humanity[2] invests Himself with man for the salvation of men,—in former times with the prophets, and now with the church. For it is fitting that like should minister to like, in order to a like salvation.

XXIV. For we were of the earth. . . . Cæsar is the prince, for the time being, whose earthly image is the old man, to which he has returned. To him, then, we are to

[1] ἄνθρωπον. [2] φιλάνθρωπος.

render the earthly things, which we bore in the image of the earthly, and the things of God to God. For each one of the passions is on us as a letter, and stamp, and sign. Now the Lord marks us with another stamp, and with other names and letters, faith instead of unbelief, and so forth. Thus we are translated from what is material to what is spiritual, "having borne the image of the heavenly" (1 Cor. xv. 49).

XXV. John says: "I indeed baptize you with water, but there cometh after me He that baptizeth with the Spirit and fire" (Matt. iii. 11). But He baptized no one with fire. But some, as Heraclius says, marked with fire the ears of those who were sealed; understanding so the apostolic saying, "For His fan is in His hand, to purge His floor: and He will gather the wheat into the garner; but the chaff He will burn with fire unquenchable."[1] There is joined, then, the expression "by fire" to that "by the Spirit;" since He separates the wheat from the chaff, that is, from the material husk, by the Spirit; and the chaff is separated, being fanned by the wind:[2] so also the Spirit possesses a power of separating material forces. Since, then, some things are produced from what is unproduced and indestructible,—that is, the germs of life,—the wheat also is stored, and the material part, as long as it is conjoined with the superior part, remains; when separated from it, it is destroyed; for it had its existence in another thing. This separating element, then, is the Spirit, and the destroying element is the fire: and material fire is to be understood. But since that which is saved is like wheat, and that which grows in the soul like chaff, and the one is incorporeal, and that which is separated is material; to the incorporeal He opposes spirit, which is rarefied and pure— almost more so than mind; and to the material [He opposes] fire, not as being evil or bad, but as strong and capable of cleansing away evil. For fire is conceived as a good force and powerful, destructive of what is baser, and conservative of what is better. Wherefore this fire is by the prophets called wise.

XXVI. Thus also, then, when God is called "a con-

[1] Matt. iii. 12.   [2] Or spirit—*πνεύματος*.

suming fire," it is because a name and sign, not of wickedness, but of power, is to be selected. For as fire is the most potent of the elements, and masters all things; so also God is all-powerful and almighty, who is able to hold, to create, to make, to nourish, to make grow, to save, having power of body and soul. As, then, fire is superior to the elements, so is the Almighty Ruler to gods, and powers, and principalities. The power of fire is twofold: one power conduces to the production and maturing of fruits and of animals, of which the sun is the image; and the other to consumption and destruction, as terrestrial fire. When, then, God is called a consuming fire, [He is called] a mighty and resistless power, to which nothing is impossible, but which is able to destroy.

Respecting such a power, also, the Saviour says, "I came to send fire upon the earth" (Luke xii. 49), indicating a power to purify what is holy, but destructive, as they say, of what is material; and, as we should say, disciplinary. Now fear pertains to fire, and diffusion to light.

XXVII. Now the more ancient men[1] did not write, as they neither wished to encroach on the time devoted to attention bestowed on what they handed down, in the way of teaching, by the additional attention bestowed on writing, nor spent the time for considering what was to be said on writing. And, perhaps convinced that the function of composition and the department of teaching did not belong to the same cast of mind, they gave way to those who had a natural turn for it. For in the case of a speaker, the stream of speech flows unchecked and impetuous, and you may catch it up hastily. But that which is always tested by readers, meeting with strict[2] examination, is thought worthy of the utmost pains, and is, so to speak, the written confirmation of [oral] instruction, and of the voice so wafted along to posterity by written composition. For that which was committed in trust to the elders, speaking in writing, uses the writer's help to hand itself down to those who are to read it. As, then, the

---

[1] πρεσβύτεροι.

[2] It seems better, with Sylb., to read ἀκριβοῦς, qualifying ἐξετάσεως (as above), than ἀκριβῶς, adv. qualifying βασανιζόμενον, tested.

magnet, repelling other matter, attracts iron alone by reason of affinity; so also books, though many read them, attract those alone who are capable of comprehending them. For the word of truth is to some "foolishness" (1 Cor. i. 18), and to others a "stumbling-block" (*ib.*); but to a few "wisdom" (*ib.*). So also is the power of God found to be. But far from the Gnostic be envy. For it is for this reason also that he asks whether it be worse to give to the unworthy, or not commit to the worthy; and runs the risk, from his abundant love of communicating, not only to every one who is qualified, but sometimes also to one unworthy, who asks importunately; not on account of his entreaty (for he loves not glory), but on account of the persistency of the petitioner who bends his mind towards faith with copious entreaty.

XXVIII. There are those calling themselves Gnostics who are envious of those in their own house more than strangers. And, as the sea is open to all, but one swims, another sails, and a third catches fish; and as the land is common, but one walks, another ploughs, another hunts,—somebody else searches the mines, and another builds a house: so also, when the Scripture is read, one is helped to faith, another to morality, and a third is freed from superstition by the knowledge of things. The athlete, who knows the Olympic stadium, strips for training, contends, and becomes victor, tripping up his antagonists who contend against his scientific method, and fighting out the contest. For scientific knowledge (γνῶσις) is necessary both for the training of the soul and for gravity of conduct; making the faithful more active and keen observers of things. For as there is no believing without elementary instruction, so neither is there comprehension without science (γνῶσις).

XXIX. For what is useful and necessary to salvation, such as [the knowledge of] the Father, and Son, and Holy Spirit, and also of our own soul, are wholly requisite; and it is at once beneficial and necessary to attain to the scientific account of them. And to those who have assumed the lead in doing good, much experience is advantageous; so that none of the things which appear to be known necessarily and eruditely by others may escape their notice. The exposition, too, of heterodox teaching affords another exercise of the inquiring soul, and keeps the disciple from being seduced from the truth, by his having already had practice beforehand in sounding all round on warlike instruments of music.

XXX. The life of the Gnostic rule, (as they say that Crete was barren of deadly animals,) is pure from every evil deed, and thought, and word; not only hating no one, but beyond envy and hatred, and all evil-speaking and slander.

XXXI. In length of days, it is not on account of his having lived long that the man is to be regarded happy, to whose lot it has also fallen, through his having lived, to be worthy of living for ever. He has pained no one, except in instructing by the word the wounded in heart, as it were by a salutary honey, which is at once sweet and pungent. So that, above all, the Gnostic preserves the decorous along with that which is in accordance with reason. For passion being cut away and stript off from the whole soul, he henceforth consorts and lives with what is noblest, which has now become pure, and emancipated to adoption.

XXXII. Pythagoras thought that he who gave things their names, ought to be regarded not only the most intelligent, but the oldest of the wise men. We must, then, search the Scriptures accurately, since they are admitted to be expressed in parables, and from the names hunt out the thoughts which the Holy Spirit, propounding respecting things, teaches by imprinting His mind, so to speak, on the expressions; that the names used with various meanings, being made the subject of accurate investigation, may be explained, and that that which is hidden under many integuments may, being handled and learned, come to light and gleam forth. For so also lead turns white as you rub it; white lead being produced from black. So also scientific knowledge (gnosis), shedding its light and brightness on things, shows itself to be in truth the divine wisdom, the pure light, which illumines the men whose eyeball is clear, unto the sure vision and comprehension of truth.

XXXIII. Lighting, then, our torch at the source of that light, by the passionate desire which has it for its object, and striving as much as possible to be assimilated to it, we become men (φῶτες) full of light (φωτός), Israelites indeed. For He called those friends and brethren who by desire and pursuit aimed after likeness to the Divinity.

XXXIV. Pure places and meadows have received voices and visions of holy phantasms. But every man who has been perfectly purified, shall be thought worthy of divine teaching and of power.

XXXV. Now I know that the mysteries of science (gnosis) are a laughing-stock to many, especially when not patched up with sophistical figurative language. And the few are at first startled at them; as when light is suddenly brought into a convivial party in the dark. Subsequently, on getting used and accustomed, and trained to reasoning, as if gladdened and exulting for delight, they [praise] the Lord. . . . For as pleasure has for its essence release from pain; so also has knowledge the removal of ignorance. For as those that are most asleep think they are most awake, being under the power of dream-visions very vivid and fixed; so those that are most ignorant think that they know most. But blessed are they who rouse themselves from this sleep and derangement, and raise their eyes to the light and the truth.

XXXVI. It is, therefore, equally requisite for him who wishes to have a pupil who is docile, and has blended faith with aspiration, to exercise himself and constantly to study by himself, investigating the truth of his speculations; and when he thinks himself right, to descend to questions regarding things contiguous. For the young birds make attempts to fly in the nest, exercising their wings.

XXXVII. For Gnostic virtue everywhere makes man good, and meek, and harmless,[1] and painless, and blessed, and ready to associate in the best way with all that is divine, in the best way with men, at once a contemplative and active divine image, and turns him into a lover of what is good by love. For what is good (τὸ καλὸν), as there it is contem-

---

[1] For ἀβλαβίς in the text, we must, translating thus, read ἀβλαβῆ. If we translate, as we may, "Gnostic virtue is a thing everywhere good, and meek," etc., no change is required in the reading.

plated and comprehended by wisdom, is here by self-control and righteousness carried into effect through faith: practising in the flesh an angelic ministry; hallowing the soul in the body, as in a place clear and stainless.

XXXVIII. Against Tatian, who says that the words, "Let there be light" (Gen. i. 3), are supplicatory. If, then, He is supplicating the supreme God, how does He say, "I am God, and beside me there is none else" (Isa. xliv. 6)? We have said that there are punishments for blasphemies, for nonsense, for outrageous expressions; which are punished and chastised by reason.

XXXIX. And he said, too, that on account of their hair and finery, women are punished by the Power that is set over these matters; which also gave to Samson strength in his hair; which punishes the women who allure to fornication through the adornment of their hair.

XL. As by the effluence of good, people are made good, in like manner are they made bad. Good is the judgment of God, and the discrimination of the believing from the unbelieving, and the judgment beforehand, so as not to fall into greater judgment—this judgment being correction.

XLI. Scripture says that infants which are exposed are delivered to a guardian angel, and that by him they are trained and reared. "And they shall be," it says, "as the faithful in this world of a hundred years of age." Wherefore also Peter, in the Revelation, says: "And a flash of fire, leaping from those infants, and striking the eyes of the women." For the just shines forth as a spark in a reed, and will judge the nations (Wisd. iii. 7).

XLII. "With the holy Thou wilt be holy" (Ps. xviii. 26). "According to thy praise is thy name glorified;" God being glorified through our knowledge, and through the inheritance. Thus also it is said, "The Lord liveth," and "The Lord hath risen" (Luke xxiv. 34).

XLIII. "A people whom I knew not hath served me" (Ps. xviii. 43);—by covenant I knew them not, alien sons, who desired what pertained to another.

XLIV. "Magnifying the salvations of His king" (Ps.

xviii. 50). All the faithful are called kings, brought to royalty through inheritance.

XLV. Long-suffering is sweetness above honey; not because it is long-suffering, but in consequence of the fruit of long-suffering. Since, then, the man of self-control is devoid of passion, inasmuch as he restrains the passions, not without toil; but when habit is formed, he is no longer a man of self-control, the man having come under the influence of one habit and of the Holy Spirit.

XLVI. The passions that are in the soul are called spirits, —not spirits of power, since in that case the man under the influence of passion would be a legion of demons; but [they are so called] in consequence of the impulse they communicate. For the soul itself, through modifications, taking on this and that other sort of qualities of wickedness, is said to receive spirits.

XLVII. The Word does not bid us renounce property;[1] but to manage property without inordinate affection; and on anything happening, not to be vexed or grieved; and not to desire to acquire. Divine Providence bids keep away from possession accompanied with passion, and from all inordinate affection, and [from this] turns back those still remaining[2] in the flesh.

XLVIII. For instance, Peter says in the Apocalypse, that abortive infants shall share the better fate;[3] that these are committed to a guardian angel, so that, on receiving knowledge, they may obtain the better abode, having had the same experiences which they would have had had they been in the body. But the others shall obtain salvation merely, as being injured and pitied, and remain without punishment, receiving this reward.

XLIX. The milk of women, flowing from the breasts and thickening, says Peter in the Apocalypse, will produce

---

[1] κτήσεως, instead of κτίσεως, as in the text, and κτῆσιν for κτίσιν in the next clause.

[2] Ἀναστρίφει ἐπὶ μόνους τοὺς ἐν σαρκί. For which, as slightly preferable, Sylburg. proposes ἔτι μένοντας ἐν σαρκί, as above.

[3] Adopting the reading μοίρας, instead of that in the text, πείρας.

minute beasts, that prey on flesh, and running back into them will consume them: teaching that punishments arise for sins. He says that they are produced from sins; as it was for their sins that the people were sold. And for their want of faith in Christ, as the apostle says, they were bitten by serpents.

L. An ancient said that the embryo is a living thing; for that the soul entering into the womb after it has been by cleansing prepared for conception, and introduced by one of the angels who preside over generation, and who knows the time for conception, moves the woman to intercourse; and that, on the seed being deposited, the spirit, which is in the seed, is, so to speak, appropriated, and is thus assumed into conjunction in the process of formation. He cited as a proof to all, how, when the angels give glad tidings to the barren, they introduce souls before conception. And in the Gospel "the babe leapt" (Luke i. 43) as a living thing. And the barren are barren for this reason, that the soul, which unites for the deposit of the seed, is not introduced so as to secure conception and generation.

LI. "The heavens declare the glory of God" (Ps. xix. 1). The heavens are taken in various meanings, both those defined by space and revolution, and those by covenant,—the immediate operation of the first-created angels. For the covenants caused a more especial appearance of angels,—that[1] in the case of Adam, that in the case of Noah, that in the case of Abraham, that in the case of Moses. For, moved by the Lord, the first-created angels exercised their influence on the angels attached to the prophets, considering the covenants the glory of God. Furthermore, the things done on earth by angels were done by the first-created angels to the glory of God.

LII. It is the Lord that is principally denominated the Heavens, and then the First-created; and after these also the holy men before the Law, as the patriarchs, and Moses, and the prophets; then also the apostles. "And the firmament showeth His handiwork." He applies the term "firmament" (στερέωμα) to God, the passionless and immoveable, as also

[1] *i.e.* the covenant.

elsewhere the same David says, "I will love Thee, O Lord, my strength (στερέωμα) and my refuge" (Ps. xviii. 1). Accordingly, the firmament itself shows forth the work of His hands,—that is, shows and manifests the work of His angels. For He shows forth and manifests those whom He hath made.

LIII. "Day unto day uttereth speech." As the heavens have various meanings, so also has day. Now speech is the Lord; and He is also frequently called day. "And night unto night showeth forth knowledge." The devil knew that the Lord was to come. But he did not believe that He was God; wherefore also he tempted Him, in order to know if He were powerful. It is said, "he left[1] Him, and departed from Him for a season;" that is, he postponed the discovery till the resurrection. For he knew that He who was to rise was the Lord. Likewise also the demons; since also they suspected that Solomon was the Lord, and they knew that he was not so, on his sinning. "Night to night." All the demons knew that He who rose after the passion was the Lord. And already Enoch had said, that the angels who transgressed taught men astronomy and divination, and the rest of the arts.

LIV. "There are no speeches or words whose voices are not heard," neither of days nor nights. "Their sound is gone forth unto all the earth." He has transferred the discourse to the saints alone, whom he calls both heavens and days.

LV. The stars, spiritual bodies, that have communications with the angels set over them, and are governed by them, are not the cause of the production of things, but are signs of what is taking place, and will take place, and have taken place in the case of atmospheric changes, of fruitfulness and barrenness, of pestilence and fevers, and in the case of men. The stars do not in the least degree exert influences, but indicate what is, and will be, and has been.

LVI. "And in the sun hath He set His tabernacle." There is a transposition here. For it is of the second coming that the discourse is. So, then, we must read what is transposed

---

[1] For ἰᾶν, which is the reading of the text, Sylburgius' suggestion of εἴα or εἴασι has been adopted.

in its due sequence: "And he, as a bridegroom issuing from his chamber, will rejoice as a giant to run his way. From heaven's end is his going forth; and there is no one who shall hide himself from his heat;" and then, "He hath set His tabernacle in the sun."

Some say that He deposited the Lord's body in the sun, as Hermogenes. And "His tabernacle," some say, is His body, others the church of the faithful.

Our Pantænus used to say, that prophecy utters its expressions indefinitely for the most part, and uses the present for the future, and again the present for the past. Which is also seen here.[1] For "He hath set" is put both for the past and the future. For the future, because, on the completion of this period, which is to run according to its present[2] constitution, the Lord will come to restore the righteous, the faithful, in whom He rests, as in a tent, to one and the same unity; for all are one body, of the same race, and have chosen the same faith and righteousness. But some as head, some as eyes, some as ears, some as hands, some as breasts, some as feet, shall be set, resplendent, in the sun. "Shine forth as the sun" (Matt. xiii. 43), or in the sun; since an angel high in command is in the sun. For he is appointed for rule over days; as the moon is for ruling over night.[3] Now angels are called days. Along with the angels in[4] the sun, it is said, they shall have assigned to them one abode, to be for some time and in some respects the sun, as it were the head of the body which is one. And, besides, they also are the rulers of the days, as that angel in the sun, for the greater purpose for which he before them[5] migrated to the same place. And again destined to ascend progressively, they reach the first abode, in accordance with the past "He hath set:" so that the first-created angels shall no

---

[1] Or rather, as Sylb. points out, this is a case of the past used for the present, etc.

[2] παρουσίαν, κατάστασιν, the reading of the text, is, as Sylburg. remarks, plainly corrupt; παροῦσαν, as above, is the most obvious correction.

[3] Gen. i. 18.   [4] μεθ' here clearly should be καθ' or ἰφ'.

[5] If we may venture to change αὐτοῦ into αὐτῶν.

longer, according to providence, exercise a definite ministry, but may be in repose, and devoted to the contemplation of God alone; while those next to them shall be promoted to the post which they have left; and so those beneath them similarly.

LVII. There are then, according to the apostle, those on the summit,[1] the first-created. And they are thrones, although Powers, being the first-created, inasmuch as God rests in them, as also in those who believe. For each one, according to his own stage of advancement, possesses the knowledge of God in a way special to himself; and in this knowledge God reposes, those who possess knowledge being made immortal by knowledge. And is not "He set His tabernacle in the sun" to be understood thus? God "set in the sun," that is, in the God who is beside Him, as in the Gospel, Eli, Eli,[2] instead of my God, my God. And what is "above all rule, and authority, and power, and every name that is named," are those from among men that are made perfect as angels and archangels, [so as to rise] to the nature of the angels first-created. For those who are changed from men to angels are instructed for a thousand years by the angels after they are brought to perfection. Then those who have taught are translated to archangelic authority; and those who have learned instruct those again who from men are changed to angels. Thus afterwards, in the prescribed periods, they are brought to the proper angelic state of the body.

LVIII. "The law of God is perfect, converting souls" (Ps. xix. 8). The Saviour Himself is called Law and Word, as Peter in "the Preaching," and the prophet: "Out of Zion shall go forth the Law, and the Word of the Lord from Jerusalem" (Isa. ii. 3).

LIX. "The testimony of the Lord is sure, making

---

[1] Ἐν τῇ ἀρχῇ ἀποκαταστάσει. The last word yields no suitable sense, and conjecture as to the right reading is vain; and we have left it untranslated. The Latin translator renders "qui in summa arce collocati sunt."

[2] Ἥλιος is (with marvellous ignorance of the Hebrew tongue, as Combefisius notices) here identified with Eli, אֵלִי.

children wise." The covenant of the Lord is true, making wise children; those free from evil, both the apostles, and then also us. Besides, the testimony of the Lord, according to which He rose again after His passion, having been verified by fact, led the church to confirmation in faith.

LX. "The fear of the Lord is pure, enduring for ever." He says that those who have been turned from fear to faith and righteousness endure for ever.

"The judgments of the Lord are true,"—sure, and incapable of being overturned; and giving rewards according to what is right, bringing the righteous to the unity of the faith. For this is shown in the words, "justified for the same."[1] "Such desires[2] are above gold and precious stone."

LXI. "For also Thy servant keeps them." Not that David alone is called servant; but the whole people saved is called the servant of God, in virtue of obedience to the command.

LXII. "Cleanse me from my secret [faults];"—thoughts contrary to right reason—defects. For He calls this foreign to the righteous man.

LXIII. "If they have not dominion over me, then shall I be innocent." If those who persecute me as they did the Lord, do not have dominion over me, I shall not be innocent. For no one becomes a martyr unless he is persecuted; nor appears righteous, unless, being wronged, he takes no revenge; nor forbearing . . . . . .

---

[1] Ps. xix. 12, Septuagint.

[2] αἱ τοιαῦται ἐπιθυμίαι, for which the Septuagint has ἐπιθυμητά, as in A. V.

FRAGMENTS

OF

CLEMENS ALEXANDRINUS.

TRANSLATED BY

REV. WILLIAM WILSON, M.A.

FRAGMENTS.

(I.)

FROM THE LATIN TRANSLATION OF CASSIODORUS.[1]

I.—COMMENTS ON THE FIRST EPISTLE OF PETER.

HAP. i. 3.—" Blessed be the God and Father of our Lord Jesus Christ, who by His great mercy hath regenerated us." For if God generated us of matter, He afterwards, by progress in life, regenerated us.

"The Father of our Lord, by the resurrection of Jesus Christ:" who, according to your faith, rises again in us; as, on the other hand, He dies in us, through the operation of our unbelief. For He said again, that the soul never returns a second time to the body in this life; and that which has become angelic does not become unrighteous or evil, so as not to have the opportunity of again sinning by the assumption of flesh; but that in the resurrection the soul[2] returns to the body, and both are joined to one another according to their peculiar nature, adapting themselves,

---

[1] Fell notes that Cassiodorus states that he had in his translation corrected what he considered erroneous in the original. Fell also is inclined to believe that these fragments are from Clement's lost work 'Υποτυπώσεις, of which he believes Adumbrationes of Cassiodorus (which we have rendered "Comments") to be a translation.

[2] "Utramque" is the reading, which is plainly corrupt. We have conjectured "animam." The rest of the sentence is so ungrammatical and' impracticable as it stands, that it is only by taking considerable liberties with it that it is translateable at all.

through the composition of each, by a kind of congruity like[1] a building of stones.

Besides, Peter says, chap. ii. 5, "Ye also, as living stones, are built up a spiritual house;" meaning the place of the angelic abode, guarded in heaven.[2] "For you," he says, "who are kept by the power of God, by faith and contemplation, to receive the end of your faith, the salvation of your souls."

Hence it appears that the soul is not naturally immortal; but is made immortal by the grace of God, through faith and righteousness, and by knowledge. "Of which salvation," he says (ver. 10), "the prophets have inquired and searched diligently," and what follows. It is declared by this that the prophets spake with wisdom, and that the Spirit of Christ was in them, according to the possession of Christ, and in subjection to Christ. For God works through archangels and kindred angels, who are called spirits of Christ.

"Which are now," he says (ver. 12), "reported unto you by them that have preached the gospel unto you." The old things which were done by the prophets and escape the observation of most, are now revealed to you by the evangelists. "For to you," he says (*ib.*), "they are manifested by the Holy Ghost, who was sent;" that is the Paraclete, of whom the Lord said, "If I go not away, He will not come" (John xvi. 7). "Unto whom" (*ib.*), it is said, "the angels desire to look;" not the apostate angels, as most suspect, but,

---

[1] The text here has "sicut sagena vel" (like a drag-net or), which we have omitted, being utterly incapable of divining any conceivable resemblance or analogy which a drag-net can afford for the re-union of the soul and body. "Sagena" is either a blunder for something else which we cannot conjecture, or the sentence is here, as elsewhere, mutilated. But it is possible that it may have been the union of the blessed to each other, and their conjunction with one another according to their affinities, which was the point handled in the original sentences, of which we have only these obscure and confusing remains.

[2] "Cœli," plainly a mistake for "cœlo" or "cœlis." There is apparently a hiatus here. "The angelic abode, guarded in heaven," most probably is the explanation of "an inheritance incorruptible and undefiled, reserved in heaven."

what is a divine truth, angels who desire to obtain the advantage of that perfection.

"By precious blood," he says (ver. 19), "as of a lamb without blemish and without spot." Here he touches on the ancient Levitical and sacerdotal celebrations; but means a soul pure through righteousness which is offered to God.

"Verily foreknown before the foundation of the world" (ver. 20). Inasmuch as He was foreknown before every creature, because He was Christ. "But manifested in the last times" by the generation of a body.

"Being born again, not of corruptible seed" (ver. 23). The soul, then, which is produced along with the body is corruptible, as some think.

"But the word of the Lord," he says (ver. 25), "endureth for ever:" as well prophecy as divine doctrine.

Chap. ii. 9.—"But ye are a chosen generation, a royal priesthood." That we are a chosen race by the election of God is abundantly clear. He says royal, because we are called to sovereignty and belong to Christ; and priesthood on account of the oblation which is made by prayers and instructions, by which are gained the souls which are offered to God.

"Who, when He was reviled," he says (ver. 23), "reviled not; when He suffered, threatened not." The Lord acted so in His goodness and patience. "But committed Himself to him that judged Him unrighteously:"[1] whether Himself, so that, regarding Himself in this way, there is a transposition.[2] He indeed gave Himself up to those who judged according to an unjust law; because He was unserviceable to them, inasmuch as He was righteous: or, He committed to God those who judged unrighteously, and without cause insisted on His death, so that they might be instructed by suffering punishment.

Chap. iii. 10.—"For he that will love life, and see good days;" that is, who wishes to become eternal and immortal. And He calls the Lord life, and the days good, that is holy.

"For the eyes of the Lord," he says, "are upon the

[1] Sic.   [2] Hyperbaton.

righteous, and His ears on their prayers:" he means the manifold inspection of the Holy Spirit. "The face of the Lord is on them that do evil" (ver. 12); that is, whether judgment, or vengeance, or manifestation.

"But sanctify the Lord Christ," he says, "in your hearts" (ver. 15). For so you have in the Lord's prayer, "Hallowed be Thy name" (Matt. vi. 9).

"For Christ," he says (ver. 18), "hath once suffered for our sins, the just for the unjust, that He might present[1] us to God; being put to death in the flesh, but quickened in the spirit." He says these things, reducing them to their faith. That is, He became alive in our spirits.

"Coming," he says (ver. 20), "He preached to those who were once unbelieving." They saw not His form, but they heard His voice.

"When the long-suffering of God" (*ib.*) holds out. God is so good, as to work the result by the teaching of salvation.

"By the resurrection," it is said (ver. 21), "of Jesus Christ:" that, namely, which is effected in us by faith.

"Angels being subjected to Him" (ver. 22), which are the first order; and "principalities" being subject, who are of the second order; and "powers" being also subject, which are said to belong to the third order.

"Who shall give account," he says, chap. iv. 5, "to Him who is ready to judge the quick and the dead."

These are trained through previous judgments (ver. 6). Therefore he adds, "For this cause was the gospel preached also to the dead"—to us, namely, who were at one time unbelievers. "That they might be judged according to men," he says, *ib.*, "in the flesh, but live according to God in the spirit." Because, that is, they have fallen away from faith; whilst they are still in the flesh they are judged according to preceding judgments, that they might repent. Accordingly, he also adds, saying, "That they might live according to God in the spirit." So Paul also; for he, too, states something of this nature when he says, "Whom I have delivered to Satan, that he might live in the spirit" (1 Cor. v. 5);

---

[1] Offerret.

that is, "as good stewards of the manifold grace of God." Similarly also Paul says, "Variously, and in many ways, God of old spake to our fathers" (Heb. i. 1).

"Rejoice," it is said (ver. 13), "that ye are partakers in the sufferings of Christ:" that is, if ye are righteous, ye suffer for righteousness' sake, as Christ suffered for righteousness. "Happy are ye, for the Spirit of God, who is the Spirit of His glory and virtue, resteth on you." This possessive "His" signifies also an angelic spirit: inasmuch as the glory of God those are, through whom, according to faith and righteousness, He is glorified, to honourable glory, according to the advancement of the saints who are brought in. "The Spirit of God on us," may be thus understood; that is, who through faith comes on the soul, like a gracefulness of mind and beauty of soul.

"Since," it is said (ver. 17), "it is time for judgment beginning at the house of God." For judgment will overtake these in the appointed persecutions.

"But the God of all grace," he says (chap. v. 10). "Of all grace," he says, because He is good, and the giver of all good things.

"Marcus, my son, saluteth you" (ver. 14). Mark, the follower of Peter, while Peter publicly preached the gospel at Rome before some of Cæsar's equites, and adduced many testimonies to Christ, in order that thereby they might be able to commit to memory what was spoken, of what was spoken by Peter, wrote entirely what is called the Gospel according to Mark. As Luke also may be recognised[1] by the style, both to have composed the Acts of the Apostles, and to have translated Paul's Epistle to the Hebrews.

II.—COMMENTS ON THE EPISTLE OF JUDE.

Jude, who wrote the catholic epistle, the brother of the sons of Joseph, and very religious, whilst knowing the near relationship of the Lord, yet did not say that he himself was

[1] The reading is "agnosceret." To yield any sense it must have been "agnoscatur" or "agnosceretur."

His brother. But what said he (ver. 1)? "Jude, a servant of Jesus Christ,"—of Him as Lord; but "the brother of James." For this is true; he was His brother, (the son)[1] of Joseph. "For (ver. 4) certain men have entered unawares, ungodly men, who had been of old ordained and predestined to the judgment of our God;" not that they might become impious, but that, being now impious, they were ordained to judgment. "For the Lord God," he says (ver. 5), "who once delivered a people out of Egypt, afterward destroyed them that believed not;" that is, that He might train them through punishment. For they were indeed punished, and they perished on account of those that are saved, until they turn to the Lord. "But the angels," he says (ver. 6), "that kept not their own pre-eminence," that, namely, which they received through advancement, "but left their own habitation," meaning, that is, the heaven and the stars, became, and are called apostates. "He hath reserved" (he says, *ib.*) "to the judgment of the great day, in chains, under darkness." He means the locality near the earth,[2] that is, the dark air. Now he called "chains" the loss of the honour in which they had stood, and the lust of feeble things; since, bound by their own lust, they cannot be converted. "As Sodom and Gomorrha," he says (ver. 7). . . . By which the Lord signifies that pardon had been granted;[3] and that on being disciplined they had repented. "Similarly[4] to the same," he says (ver. 8), "also those dreamers,"—that is, who dream in their imagination lusts and wicked desires, regarding as good not that which is truly good, and superior to all good,—"defile the flesh, despise dominion, and speak evil of majesty," that is, the only Lord,[5] who is truly our Lord, Jesus Christ, and alone worthy of praise. They "speak evil of majesty," that is, of the angels.

---

[1] "Son" supplied.   [2] Terris.

[3] "Quibus significat Dominus remissius esse," the reading here, defies translation and emendation. We suppose a hiatus here, and change "remissius" into "remissum" to get the above sense. The statement cannot apply to Sodom and Gomorrha.

[4] Similiter iisdem.

[5] Dominus—Dominium, referring to the clause "despise dominion."

"When Michael, the archangel (ver. 9), disputing with the devil, debated about the body of Moses." Here he confirms the assumption of Moses. He is here called Michael, who through an angel near to us debated with the devil.

"But these," he says (ver. 10), "speak evil of those things which they know not; but what they know naturally, as brute beasts, in these things they corrupt themselves." He means that they eat, and drink, and indulge in uncleanness, and says that they do other things that are common to them with animals, devoid of reason.

"Woe unto them!" he says (ver. 11), "for they have gone in the way of Cain." For so also we lie under Adam's sin through similarity of sin. "Clouds," he says (ver. 12), "without water; who do not possess in themselves the divine and fruitful word." Wherefore, he says, "men of this kind are carried about both by winds and violent blasts."[1] "Trees," he says, "of autumn, without fruit,"— unbelievers, that is, who bear no fruit of fidelity. "Twice dead," he says: once, namely, when they sinned by transgressing, and a second time when delivered up to punishment, according to the predestined judgments of God; inasmuch as it is to be reckoned death, even when each one does not forthwith deserve the inheritance. "Waves," he says (ver. 13), "of a raging sea." By these words he signifies the life of the Gentiles, whose end is abominable ambition.[2] "Wandering stars,"—that is, he means those who err and are apostates are of that kind of stars which fell from the seats of the angels,—" to whom," for their apostasy, "the blackness of darkness is reserved for ever. Enoch also, the seventh from Adam," he says (ver. 14), "prophesied of these." In these words he verifies the prophecy.

"Those," he says (ver. 19), "separating" the faithful from the unfaithful, being convicted according to their own unbelief.

[1] Spiritibus.
[2] The reading "vitam Gentilem significat quorum ambitionis abominabilis est finis," is manifestly corrupt. "The end of whose ambition is abominable" would be obtained by a slighter change than what is given above.

And again those separating from the flesh.[1] He says, "Animal[2] not having the spirit;" that is, the spirit which is by faith, which supervenes through the practice of righteousness.

"But ye, beloved," he says (ver. 20), "building up yourselves on your most holy faith, in the Holy Spirit." "But some," he says (ver. 21), "save, plucking them from the fire" (ver. 22); "but of some have compassion in fear," that is, teach those who fall into the fire to free themselves. "Hating," he says (ver. 23), "that spotted garment, which is carnal:" that of the soul, namely; the spotted garment is a spirit polluted by carnal lusts.[3]

"Now to Him," he says (ver. 24), "who is able to keep you without stumbling, and present you faultless before the presence of His glory in joy." In the presence of His glory: he means in the presence of the angels, to be presented faultless, having become angels.[4] When Daniel speaks of the people and comes into the presence of the Lord, he does not say this, because he saw God: for it is impossible that any one whose heart is not pure should see God; but he says this, that everything that the people did was in the sight of God, and was manifest to Him; that is, that nothing is hid from the Lord.

Now, in the Gospel according to Mark, the Lord being interrogated by the chief of the priests if He was the Christ, the son of the blessed God, answering, said, "I am;[5] and ye shall see the Son of man sitting at the right hand of power."[6] But powers[7] mean the holy angels. Further, when He says "at the right hand of God," He means the self-same [beings], by reason of the equality and likeness of the angelic

---

[1] "Discernentes a carnibus,"—a sentence which has got either displaced or corrupted, or both.

[2] Animales.

[3] By a slight change of punctuation, and by substituting "maculata" for "macula," we get the sense as above. "Animæ videlicet tunica macula est," is the reading of the text.

[4] We have here with some hesitation altered the punctuation. In the text, "To be presented" begins a new sentence.

[5] Mark xiv. 62. There is blundering here as to the differences between the evangelists' accounts, as a comparison of them shows.

[6] Virtutis.   [7] Virtutes.

and holy powers, which are called by the name of God. He says, therefore, that He sits at the right hand; that is, that He rests in pre-eminent honour. In the other Gospels, however, He is said not to have replied to the high priest, on his asking if He was the Son of God. But what said He? "You say."[1] Answering sufficiently well. For had He said, It is as you understand, he would have said what was not true, not confessing Himself to be the Son of God; [for] they did not entertain this opinion of Him; but by saying "You say,"[2] He spake truly. For what they had no knowledge of, but expressed in words, that He confessed to be true.

III.—COMMENTS ON THE FIRST EPISTLE OF JOHN.

Chap. i. 1. "That which was from the beginning; which we have seen with our eyes; which we have heard."

Following the Gospel according to John, and in accordance with it, this Epistle also contains the spiritual principle.

What therefore he says, "from the beginning," the Presbyter explained to this effect, that the beginning of generation is not separated from the beginning of the Creator. For when he says, "That which was from the beginning," he touches upon the generation without beginning of the Son, who is co-existent with the Father. There was, then, a Word importing an unbeginning eternity; as also the Word itself, that is, the Son of God, who being, by equality of substance, one with the Father, is eternal and uncreate. That He was always the Word, is signified by saying, "In the beginning was the Word." But by the expression, "we have seen with our eyes," he signifies the Lord's presence in the flesh, "and our hands have handled," he says, "of the Word of life." He means not only His flesh, but the virtues of the Son, like the sunbeam which penetrates to the lowest places, —this sunbeam coming in the flesh became palpable to the disciples. It is accordingly related in traditions, that John,

---

[1] Matt. xxvi. 64: "Thou hast said: nevertheless, I say unto you, Hereafter ye shall see the Son of man sitting on the right hand of power, and coming in the clouds of heaven."

[2] *i.e.* It is as you say.

touching the outward body itself, sent his hand deep down into it, and that the solidity of the flesh offered no obstacle, but gave way to the hand of the disciple.

"And our hands have handled of the Word of life;" that is, He who came in the flesh became capable of being touched. As also,

Ver. 2. "The life was manifested." For in the Gospel he thus speaks: "And what was made, in Him was life, and the life was the light of men" (John i. 3, 4).

"And we show unto you that eternal life, which was with the Father, and was manifested unto you."

He signifies by the appellation of Father, that the Son also existed always, without beginning.

Ver. 5. "For God," he says, "is light."

He does not express the divine essence, but wishing to declare the majesty of God, he has applied to the Divinity what is best and most excellent in the view of men. Thus also Paul, when he speaks of "light inaccessible" (1 Tim. vi. 16). But John himself also in this same Epistle says, "God is love" (1 John iv. 16): pointing out the excellencies of God, that He is kind and merciful; and because He is light, makes men righteous, according to the advancement of the soul, through charity. God, then, who is ineffable in respect of His substance, is light.

"And in Him is no darkness at all,"—that is, no passion, no keeping up of evil respecting any one, [He] destroys no one, but gives salvation to all. Light moreover signifies, either the precepts of the Law, or faith, or doctrine. Darkness is the opposite of these things. Not as if there were another way; since there is only one way according to the divine precepts. For the work of God is unity. Duality and all else that exists, except unity, arises from perversity of life.

Ver. 7. "And the blood of Jesus Christ His Son," he says, "cleanses us." For the doctrine of the Lord, which is very powerful, is called His blood.

Ver. 10. "If we say that we have not sinned, we make Him a liar, and His word is not in us." His doctrine, that is, or word is truth.

Chap. ii. 1. "And if any man sin," he says, "we have an advocate[1] with the Father, Jesus Christ." For so the Lord is an advocate with the Father for us. So also is there an advocate, whom, after His assumption, He vouchsafed to send. For these primitive and first-created virtues are unchangeable as to substance, and along with subordinate angels and archangels, whose names they share, effect divine operations. Thus also Moses names the virtue of the angel Michael, by an angel near to himself and of lowest grade. The like also we find in the holy prophets; but to Moses an angel appeared near and at hand. Moses heard him and spoke to him, manifestly, face to face. On the other prophets, through the agency of angels, an impression was made, as of beings hearing and seeing.

On this account also, they alone heard, and they alone saw; as also is seen in the case of Samuel (1 Sam. iii. 3). Elisæus also alone heard the voice by which he was called (1 Kings xix.). If the voice had been open and common, it would have been heard by all. In this instance it was heard by him alone, in whom the impression made by the angel worked.

Ver. 2. "And not only for our sins,"—that is, for those of the faithful,—is the Lord the propitiator, does he say, "but also for the whole world." He, indeed, saves all; but some [He saves], converting them by punishments; others, however, who follow voluntarily [He saves] with dignity of honour; so "that every knee should bow to Him, of things in heaven, and things on earth, and things under the earth" (Phil. ii. 10); that is, angels, men, and souls that before His advent have departed from this temporal life.

Ver. 3. "And by this we know that we know Him, if we keep His commandments." For the Gnostic[2] [he who knows] also does the works which pertain to the province of virtue. But he who performs the works is not necessarily also a Gnostic. For a man may be a doer of right works, and yet not a knower of the mysteries of science. Finally, knowing that some works are performed from fear of punish-

[1] Consolatorem.   [2] "Intellector" in Latin translation.

ment, and some on account of the promise of reward, he shows the perfection of the man gifted with knowledge, who fulfils his works by love. Further, he adds, and says:

Ver. 5. "But whoso keepeth His word, in him verily is the love of God perfected: hereby know we that we are in Him,"—by faith and love.

Ver. 7. "I write no new commandment unto you, but an old commandment, which ye had from the beginning,"—through the Law, that is, and the prophets; where it is said, God is one. Accordingly, also, he infers, "For the old commandment is the word which ye have heard."

Again, however, he says:

Ver. 8. "This is the commandment; for the darkness" of perversion, that is, "has passed away, and, lo, the true light hath already shone,"—that is, through faith, through knowledge, through the Covenant working in men, through prepared judgments.

Ver. 9. "He that saith he is in the light,"—in the light, he means in the truth,—"and hateth," he says, "his brother." By his brother, he means not only his neighbour, but also the Lord. For unbelievers hate Him and do not keep His commandments. Therefore also he infers:

Ver. 10. "He that loveth his brother abideth in the light; and there is none occasion of stumbling in him."

Vers. 12–14. He then indicates the stages of advancement and progress of souls that are still located in the flesh; and calls those whose sins have been forgiven, for the Lord's name's sake, "little children," for many believe on account of the name only. He styles "fathers" the perfect, "who have known what was from the beginning," and received with understanding,—the Son, that is, of whom he said above, "that which was from the beginning."

"I write," says he, "to you, young men, because ye have overcome the wicked one." Young men strong in despising pleasures. "The wicked one" points out the eminence of the devil. "The children," moreover, know the Father; having fled from idols and gathered together to the one God.

Ver. 13. "For the world," he says, "is in the wicked one."

Is not the world, and all that is in the world, called God's creation and very good? Yes. But,

Ver. 16. "The lust of the flesh, the lust of the eyes, and the ambition of the world," which arise from the perversion of life, "are not of the Father, but of the world," and of you.

Ver. 17. "Therefore also the world shall pass away, and the lust thereof; but he that doeth the will of God" and His commandments "abideth for ever."

Ver. 19. "They went out from us; but they were not of us"—neither the apostate angels, nor men falling away;— "but that they may be manifested that they are not of us." With sufficient clearness he distinguishes the class of the elect and that of the lost, and that which remaining in faith "has an unction from the Holy One," which comes through faith. He that abideth not in faith.

Ver. 22. "A liar" and "an antichrist, who denieth that Jesus is the Christ." For Jesus, Saviour and Redeemer, is also Christ the King.

Ver. 23. "He who denies the Son," by ignoring Him, "has not the Father, nor does he know Him." But he who knoweth the Son and the Father, knows according to knowledge, and when the Lord shall be manifested at His second advent, shall have confidence and not be confounded. Which confusion is heavy punishment.

Ver. 29. "Every one," he says, "who doeth righteousness is born of God;" being regenerated, that is, according to faith.

Chap. iii. 1. "For the world knoweth us not, as it knew Him not." He means by the world those who live a worldly life in pleasures.

Ver. 2. "Beloved," says he, "now are we the sons of God," not by natural affection, but because we have God as our Father. For it is the greater love that, seeing we have no relationship to God, He nevertheless loves us and calls us His sons. "And it hath not yet appeared what we shall be;" that is, to what kind of glory we shall attain. "For if He shall be manifested,"—that is, if we are made perfect,—"we shall be like Him," as reposing and justified, pure in virtue, "so that we may see Him" (His countenance) "as He is," by comprehension.

Ver. 8. "He that doeth unrighteousness is of the devil," that is, of the devil as his father, following and choosing the same things. "The devil sinneth from the beginning," he says. From the beginning from which he began to sin, incorrigibly persevering in sinning.

Ver. 9. He says, "Whosoever is born of God does not commit sin, for His seed remaineth in him;" that is, His word in him who is born again through faith.

Ver. 10. "Thus we know the children of God, as likewise the children of the devil," who choose things like the devil; for so also they are said to be of the wicked one.

Ver. 15. "Every one who hateth his brother is a murderer." For in him through unbelief Christ dies. Rightly, therefore, he continues, "And ye know that no murderer and unbeliever hath eternal life abiding in him." For the living Christ[1] abides in the believing soul.

Ver. 16. "For He Himself laid down His life for us;" that is, for those who believe; that is, for the apostles. If then He laid down His life for the apostles, he means His apostles themselves: as if he said, We, I say, the apostles, for whom He laid down His life, "ought to lay down our lives for the brethren;" for the salvation of their neighbours was the glory of the apostles.

Ver. 20. He says, "For God is greater than our heart;" that is, the virtue of God [is greater] than conscience, which will follow the soul. Wherefore he continues, and says, "and knoweth all things."

Ver. 21. "Beloved, if our heart condemn us not, it will have confidence before God."

Ver. 24. "And hereby we know that He dwelleth in us by His Spirit, which He hath given us;" that is, by superintendence and foresight of future events.

Chap. iv. 18. He says, "Perfect love casteth out fear." For the perfection of a believing man is love.

[1] The text reads "Christi," which yields no suitable sense, and for which we have substituted "Christus."

Chap. v. 6. He says, "This is He who came by water and blood;" and again,—

Ver. 7. "For there are three that bear witness, the Spirit," which is life, "and the water," which is regeneration and faith, "and the blood," which is knowledge; "and these three are one." For in the Saviour are those saving virtues, and life itself exists in His own Son.

Ver. 14. "And this is the confidence which we have towards Him, that if we ask anything according to His will, He will hear us." He does not say absolutely what we shall ask, but what we ought to ask.

Ver. 19. "And the whole world lieth in the wicked one;" not the creation, but worldly men, and those who live according to their lusts.

Ver. 20. "And the Son of God hath come and given us understanding," which comes to us, that is, by faith, and is also called the Holy Spirit.

IV.—COMMENTS ON THE SECOND EPISTLE OF JOHN.

The second Epistle of John, which is written to Virgins, is very simple. It was written to a Babylonian lady, by name Electa, and indicates the election of the holy church. He establishes in this Epistle that the following out of the faith is not without charity, and so that no one divide Jesus Christ; but only to believe that Jesus Christ has come in the flesh. For he who has the Son by apprehension in his intellect knows also the Father, and grasps with his mind intelligibly the greatness of His power working without beginning of time.

Ver. 10. He says, "If any come unto you and bring not this doctrine, receive him not into your house, neither bid him God speed; for he that biddeth him God speed is partaker of his evil deeds." He forbids us to salute such, and to receive them to our hospitality. For this is not harsh in the case of a man of this sort. But he admonishes them neither to confer nor dispute with such as are not able to handle divine things with intelligence, lest through them they be seduced from the doctrine of truth, influenced by plausible reasons. Now, I think that we are not even to pray with such, because in the prayer which is made at home, after rising from prayer, the salutation of joy is also the token of peace.

(II.)

FROM NICETAS BISHOP OF HERACLEA'S CATENA.

I.—JOB I. 21.

But Job's words may be more elegantly understood thus: "Naked" of evil and sin was I formed from the earth at the beginning, as if from a "mother's womb: naked to the earth shall I also depart;" naked,[1] not of possessions, for that were a trivial and common thing, but of evil and sin, and of the unsightly shape which follows those who have led bad lives. Obviously, all of us human beings are born naked, and again are buried naked, swathed only in grave-clothes. For God hath provided for us another life, and made the present life the way for the course which leads to it; appointing the supplies derived from what we possess merely as provisions for the way; and on our quitting this way, the wealth, consisting of the things which we possessed, journeys no farther with us. For not a single thing that we possess is properly our own: of one possession alone, that is godliness, are we properly owners. Of this, death, when it overtakes us, will not rob us; but from all else it will eject us, though against our will. For it is for the support of life that we all have received what we possess; and after enjoying merely the use of it, each one departs, obtaining from life a brief remembrance. For this is the end of all prosperity; this is the conclusion of the good things of this life. Well, then, does the infant, on opening its eyes, after issuing from the womb, im-

[1] This down to "lives" is quoted, *Miscellanies*, book iv. ch. xxv. p. 214, vol. ii. Ante-Nicene Library.

mediately begin with crying, not with laughter. For it weeps, as if bewailing life, at whose hands from the outset it tastes of deadly gifts. For immediately on being born its hands and feet are swaddled; and swathed in bonds it takes the breast. O introduction to life, precursor of death! The child has but just entered on life, and straightway there is put upon it the raiment of the dead: for nature reminds those that are born of their end. Wherefore also the child, on being born, wails, as if crying plaintively to its mother. Why, O mother, didst thou bring me forth to this life, in which prolongation of life is progress to death? Why hast thou brought me into this troubled world, in which, on being born, swaddling bands are my first experience? Why hast thou delivered me to such a life as this, in which both a pitiable youth wastes away before old age, and old age is shunned as under the doom of death? Dreadful, O mother, is the course of life, which has death as the goal of the runner. Bitter is the road of life we travel, with the grave as the wayfarer's inn. Perilous the sea of life we sail; for it has Hades as a pirate to attack us. Man alone is born in all respects naked, without a weapon or clothing born with him; not as being inferior to the other animals, but that nakedness and your bringing nothing with you may produce thought; and that thought may bring out dexterity, expel sloth, introduce the arts for the supply of our needs, and beget variety of contrivances. For, naked, man is full of contrivances, being pricked on by his necessity, as by a goad, how to escape rains, how to elude cold, how to fence off blows, how to till the earth, how to terrify wild beasts, how to subdue the more powerful of them. Wetted with rain, he contrived a roof; having suffered from cold, he invented clothing; being struck, he constructed a breastplate; bleeding his hands with the thorns in tilling the ground, he availed himself of the help of tools; in his naked state liable to become a prey to wild beasts, he discovered from his fear an art which frightened what frightened him. Nakedness begat one accomplishment after another; so that even his nakedness was a gift and a master-favour. Accordingly, Job also being made naked of wealth, possessions, of the blessing of children, of a numerous offspring, and having lost everything in a short time, uttered this grateful exclamation: "Naked came I out of the womb, naked also shall I depart thither;"—to God, that is, and to that blessed lot and rest.

II.—FROM THE SAME.

Job xxiv. 7. Calmness is a thing which, of all other things, is most to be prized. As an example of this, the word proposes to us the blessed Job. For it is said of him, "What man is like Job, who drinketh up scorning like water?" For truly enviable, and, in my judgment, worthy of all admiration, a man is, if he has attained to such a degree of long-suffering as to be able with ease to grapple with the pain, truly keen, and not easily conquered by everybody, which arises from being wronged.

III.—FROM NICETAS' CATENA ON MATTHEW.

Matt. v. 42. Alms are to be given, but with judgment, and to the deserving, that we may obtain a recompense from the Most High. But woe to those who have and who take under false pretences, or who are able to help themselves and want to take from others. For he who has, and, to carry out false pretences or out of laziness, takes, shall be condemned.

IV.—FROM THE SAME.

Matt. xiii. 31, 32. The word which proclaims the kingdom of heaven is sharp and pungent as mustard, and represses bile, that is, anger, and checks inflammation, that is, pride; and from this word the soul's true health and eternal soundness[1] flow. To such increased size did the growth of the word come, that the tree which sprang from it (that is, the Church of Christ established over the whole earth) filled the world, so that the fowls of the air—that is, divine angels and lofty souls—dwelt in its branches.

[1] εὐκρασία.

V.—FROM THE SAME.

Matt. xii. 46. A pearl, and that pellucid and of purest ray, is Jesus, whom of the lightning flash of Divinity the Virgin bore. For as the pearl, produced in flesh and the oyster-shell and moisture, appears to be a body moist and transparent, full of light and spirit; so also God the Word, incarnate, is intellectual light,[1] sending His rays, through a body luminous and moist.

(III.)

FROM THE CATENA ON LUKE, EDITED BY CORDERIUS.

Luke iii. 22. God here assumed the "likeness" not of a man, but "of a dove," because He wished, by a new apparition of the Spirit in the likeness of a dove, to declare His simplicity and majesty.

Luke xvi. 17. Perhaps by the iota and tittle His righteousness cries, "If ye come right unto me, I will also come right to you; but if crooked, I also will come crooked, saith the Lord of hosts;" intimating that the ways of sinners are intricate and crooked. For the way right and agreeable to nature which is intimated by the iota of Jesus, is His goodness, which constantly directs those who believe from hearing. "There shall not, therefore, pass from the law one iota or one tittle," neither from the right and good the mutual promises, nor from the crooked and unjust the punishment assigned to them. "For the Lord doeth good to the good, but those who turn aside into crooked ways God will lead with the workers of iniquity" (Ps. cxxv. 4).

[1] φωτός here has probably taken the place of φωτεινοῦ.

(IV.)

FROM THE BOOKS OF THE HYPOTYPOSES.

FROM BOOK III.—IN ŒCUMENIUS ON 1 COR. XI. 10.

"Because of the angels." By the angels he means righteous and virtuous men. Let her be veiled then, that she may not lead them to stumble into fornication. For the real angels in heaven see her though veiled.

BOOK IV.—IN THE SAME ON 2 COR. V. 16.

"And if we have known Christ after the flesh." As "after the flesh" in our case is being in the midst of sins, and being out of them is "not after the flesh;" so also "after the flesh" in the case of Christ was His subjection to natural affections, and His not being subject to them is to be "not after the flesh." But, he says, as He was released, so also are we.

BOOK IV.—IN THE SAME ON 2 COR. VI. 11.

"Our heart is enlarged," to teach you all things. But ye are straitened in your own bowels, that is, in love to God, in which ye ought to love me.

FROM BOOK V.—IN THE SAME ON GAL. V. 24.

"And they that are Christ's [have crucified] the flesh." And why mention one aspect of virtue after another? For there are some who have crucified themselves as far as the passions are concerned, and the passions as far as respects themselves. According to this interpretation the "and" is not superfluous. "And they that are Christ's"—that is, striving after Him—"have crucified their own flesh."

FROM BOOK V.—IN MOSCHUS' SPIRITUAL MEADOW, CHAP. 176.

Yes, truly, the apostles were baptized, as Clement the Stromatist relates in the fifth book of the Hypotyposes. For, in explaining the apostolic statement, "I thank God that I baptized none of you," he says, Christ is said to have baptized Peter alone, and Peter Andrew, and Andrew John, and they James and the rest.

FROM BOOK VI.—IN EUSEBIUS' ECCLESIASTICAL HISTORY, II. 1.

Now Clement, writing in the sixth book of the Hypotyposes, makes this statement. For he says that Peter and James and John, after the Saviour's ascension, though pre-eminently honoured by the Lord, did not contend for glory, but made James the Just, bishop of Jerusalem.

FROM THE SAME.—IN EUSEBIUS' ECCLESIASTICAL HISTORY, II. 15.

So, then, through the visit of the divine word to them, the power of Simon was extinguished, and immediately was destroyed along with the man himself. And such a ray of godliness shone forth on the minds of Peter's hearers, that they were not satisfied with the once hearing or with the unwritten teaching of the divine proclamation, but with all manner of entreaties importuned Mark, to whom the Gospel is ascribed, he being the companion of Peter, that he would leave in writing a record of the teaching which had been delivered to them verbally; and did not let the man alone till they prevailed upon him; and so to them we owe the scripture called the "Gospel by Mark." On learning what had been done, through the revelation of the Spirit, it is said that the apostle was delighted with the enthusiasm of the men, and sanctioned the composition for reading in the churches. Clemens gives the narrative in the sixth book of the Hypotyposes.

FROM THE SAME.—IN EUSEBIUS, IBID.

Then, also, as the divine Scripture says, Herod, on the execution of James, seeing that what was done pleased the Jews, laid hands also on Peter; and having put him in chains, would have presently put him to death, had not an angel in a divine vision appeared to him by night, and wondrously releasing him from his bonds, sent him away to the ministry of preaching.

FROM THE SAME.—IN EUSEBIUS' ECCLESIASTICAL HISTORY, VI. 14.

And in the Hypotyposes, in a word, he has made abbreviated narratives of the whole testamentary Scripture; and has not passed over the disputed books,—I mean Jude and the rest of the Catholic Epistles and Barnabas, and what is called the Revelation of Peter. And he says that the Epistle to the Hebrews is Paul's, and was written to the Hebrews in the Hebrew language; but that Luke, having carefully translated it, gave it to the Greeks, and hence the same colouring in the expression is discoverable in this epistle and the Acts; and that the name " Paul an apostle " was very properly not prefixed, for, he says, that writing to the Hebrews, who were prejudiced against him and suspected, he with great wisdom did not repel them in the beginning by putting down his name.

FROM BOOK VII.

1 Tim. ii. 6. "In his times;" that is, when men were in a condition of fitness for faith.

1 Tim. iii. 16. " Was seen of angels." O mystery! The angels saw Christ while He was with us, not having seen Him before. Not as by men.

1 Tim. v. 8. "And especially those of his own house." He provides for his own and those of his own house, who not only provides for his relatives, but also for himself, by extirpating the passions.

1 Tim. v. 10. "If she have washed the feet of saints;" that is, if she has performed without shame the meanest offices for the saints.

1 Tim. v. 21. "Without prejudice;"[1] that is, without falling under the doom and punishment of disobedience through making any false step.

1 Tim. vi. 13. "Who witnessed before Pontius Pilate." For He testified by what he did that He was Christ the Son of God.

2 Tim. ii. 2. "By many witnesses;"[2] that is, the law and the prophets. For there the apostle made witnesses of his own preaching.

BOOK VII.—IN EUSEBIUS' ECCLESIASTICAL HISTORY, II. 1.

To James the Just, and John and Peter, the Lord after His resurrection imparted knowledge (τὴν γνῶσιν). These imparted it to the rest of the apostles, and the rest of the apostles to the Seventy, of whom Barnabas was one.

IN THE SAME, II. 2.

And of this James, Clement also relates an anecdote worthy of remembrance in the seventh book of the Hypotyposes, from a tradition of his predecessors. He says that the man who brought him to trial, on seeing him bear his testimony, was moved, and confessed that he was a Christian himself. Accordingly, he says, they were both led away together, and on the way the other asked James to forgive him. And he, considering a little, said, "Peace be to thee," and kissed him. And so both were beheaded together.

SAME, VI. 14.

And now, as the blessed Presbyter used to say, since the Lord, as the Apostle of the Almighty, was sent to the

---

[1] προκρίματος, "without preferring one before another."—A. V.
[2] διά. A. V. "before."

Hebrews, Paul, as having been sent to the Gentiles, did not subscribe himself apostle of the Hebrews, out of modesty and reverence for the Lord, and because, being the herald and apostle of the Gentiles, his writing to the Hebrews was something over and above [his assigned function].

SAME.

Again, in the same books Clement has set down a tradition which he had received from the elders before him, in regard to the order of the Gospels, to the following effect. He says that the Gospels containing the genealogies were written first, and that the Gospel according to Mark was composed under the following circumstances:

Peter having preached the word publicly at Rome, and by the Spirit proclaimed the gospel, those who were present, who were numerous, entreated Mark, inasmuch as he had attended him from an early period, and remembered what had been said, to write down what had been spoken. On his composing the Gospel, he handed it to those who had made the request to him; which coming to Peter's knowledge, he neither hindered nor encouraged. But John, the last of all, seeing that what was corporeal was set forth in the Gospels, on the entreaty of his intimate friends, and inspired by the Spirit, composed a spiritual Gospel.

(V.)

FROM THE BOOK ON PROVIDENCE.

IN S. MAXIMUS, VOL. II. 114.

Being is in God. God is divine being, eternal and without beginning, incorporeal and illimitable, and the cause of what exists. Being is that which wholly subsists. Nature is the truth of things, or the inner reality of them. According to others, it is the production of what has come to existence; and according to others, again, it is the providence of God, causing the being, and the manner of being, in the things which are produced.

IN THE SAME, P. 152.

Willing is a natural power, which desires what is in accordance with nature. Willing is a natural appetency, corresponding with the nature of the rational creature. Willing is a natural spontaneous movement of the self-determining mind, or the mind voluntarily moved about anything. Spontaneity is the mind moved naturally, or an intellectual self-determining movement of the soul.

(VI.)

FROM THE BOOK "ON THE SOUL."

FOUND IN MAXIMUS, SERMON 53, "ON THE SOUL," P. 156, AND ANTONIUS MELISSA.

Souls that breathe free of all things, possess life, and though separated from the body, and found possessed of a longing for it, are borne immortal to the bosom of God: as in the winter season the vapours of the earth attracted by the sun's rays rise to him.

FOUND IN THE BAROCC MS. 143, FOL. 181, P. 1, CHAPTER "ON CARE FOR THE SOUL."

All souls are immortal, even those of the wicked, for whom it were better that they were not deathless. For, punished with the endless vengeance of quenchless fire, and not dying, it is impossible for them to have a period put to their misery.

(VII.)

FRAGMENT FROM THE BOOK "ON SLANDER."

IN ANTONIUS MELISSA, B. II. SERM. 69, ON "SLANDERERS AND INSULT."[1]

Never be afraid of the slanderer who addresses you. But rather say, Stop, brother; I daily commit more grievous errors, and how can I judge him? For you will gain two things, healing with one plaster both yourself and your neighbour. He shows what is really evil. Whence, by these arguments, God has contrived to make each one's disposition manifest.

MAXIMUS, SERMON 59, P. 669; JOHN OF DAMASCUS, B. II.; ANTONIUS MELISSA, B. I. SERM. 64, AND B. II. SERM. 87.

It is not abstaining from deeds that justifies the believer, but purity and sincerity of thoughts.

(VIII.)

OTHER FRAGMENTS FROM ANTONIUS MELISSA.

BOOK I. SERMON 17, "ON CONFESSION."

Repentance then becomes capable of wiping out every sin, when on the occurrence of the soul's fault it admits no delay, and does not let the impulse pass on to a long space of time. For it is in this way that evil will be unable to leave a trace in us, being plucked away at the moment of its assault like a newly planted plant.

As the creatures called crabs are easy to catch, from their going sometimes forward and sometimes backward; so also

---

[1] The evidence on which this is ascribed to Clement is very slender.

the soul, which at one time is laughing, at another weeping, and at another giving way to luxury, can do no good.

He who is sometimes grieving, and is sometimes enjoying himself and laughing, is like a man stoning the dog of voluptuousness with bread, who chases it in appearance, but in fact invites it to remain near him.

BOOK I. SERMON 51, ON PRAISE.

Some flatterers were congratulating a wise man. He said to them, If you stop praising me, I think myself something great after your departure; but if you do not stop praising me, I guess my own impurity.

Feigned praise is worth less than true censure.

BOOK II. SERMON 46, ON THE LAZY AND INDOLENT.

To the weak and infirm, what is moderate appears excessive.

BOOK II. SERMON 55, ON YOUR NEIGHBOUR—THAT YOU ARE TO BEAR HIS BURDENS, ETC.

The reproof that is given with knowledge is very faithful. Sometimes also the knowledge of those who are condemned is found to be the most perfect demonstration.

BOOK II. SERMON 74, ON THE PROUD, AND THOSE DESIROUS OF VAINGLORY.

To the man who exalts and magnifies himself is attached the quick transition and the fall to low estate, as the divine word teaches.

BOOK II. SERMON 87.

Pure speech and a spotless life are the throne and true temple of God.

(IX.)

FRAGMENT OF THE TREATISE ON MARRIAGE.

**MAXIMUS, SERMON III. P. 538, ON MODESTY AND CHASTITY.
—JOHN OF DAMASCUS, BOOK III.—PARALLEL CHAP. 27.**

It is not only fornication, but also the giving in marriage prematurely, that is called fornication; when, so to speak, one not of ripe age is given to a husband, either of her own accord or by her parents.

(X.)

FRAGMENTS OF OTHER LOST BOOKS.

**MAXIMUS, SERMON 2.—JOHN OF DAMASCUS, II. CHAP. 70.—
ANTONIUS MELISSA, BOOK I. SERMON 52.**

Flattery is the bane of friendship. Most men are accustomed to pay court to the good fortune of princes, rather than to the princes themselves.

MAXIMUS, SERMON 13, P. 574.—ANTONIUS MELISSA, SERMON 32, P. 45, AND SERMON 33, P. 57.

The lovers of frugality shun luxury as the bane of soul and body. The possession and use of necessaries has nothing injurious in quality, but it has in quantity above measure. Scarcity of food is a necessary benefit.

**MAXIMUS, SERMON 52, P. 654.—ANTONIUS MELISSA,
BOOK I. SERMON 54.**

The vivid remembrance of death is a check upon diet; and when the diet is lessened, the passions are diminished along with it.

MAXIMUS, SERMON 55, P. 661.

Above all, Christians are not allowed to correct with violence the delinquencies of sins. For it is not those that abstain from wickedness from compulsion, but those that abstain from choice, that God crowns. It is impossible for a man to be steadily good except by his own choice. For he that is made good by compulsion of another is not good; for he is not what he is by his own choice. For it is the freedom of each one that makes true goodness and reveals real wickedness. Whence through these dispositions God contrived to make His own disposition manifest.

(XI.)

FRAGMENTS FOUND IN GREEK ONLY IN THE OXFORD EDITION.

FROM THE LOST WORK "ON THE PASSOVER."

Quoted in the Paschal Chronicle.

Accordingly, in the years gone by, Jesus went to eat the passover sacrificed by the Jews, keeping the feast. But when He had preached, He who was the Passover, the Lamb of God, led as a sheep to the slaughter, presently taught His disciples the mystery of the type on the thirteenth day, on which also they inquired, "Where wilt Thou that we prepare for Thee to eat the passover?" (Matt. xxvi. 17.) It was on this day, then, that both the consecration of the unleavened bread and the preparation for the feast took place. Whence John naturally describes the disciples as already previously prepared to have their feet washed by the Lord. And on the following day our Saviour suffered, He who was the Passover,—propitiously sacrificed by the Jews.

THE SAME.

Suitably, therefore, to the fourteenth day, on which He

also suffered, in the morning, the chief priests and the scribes, who brought Him to Pilate, did not enter the Prætorium, that they might not be defiled, but might freely eat the passover in the evening. With this precise determination of the days both the whole Scriptures agree, and the Gospels harmonize. The resurrection also attests it. He certainly rose on the third day, which fell on the first day of the weeks of harvest, on which the law prescribed that the priest should offer up the sheaf.

PARABLE OF THE PRODIGAL SON, LUKE XI., IN MACARIUS CHRYSOCEPHALUS' ORATION ON LUKE XI., TOWARDS THE CLOSE.

What choral dance and high festival is held in heaven, if there is one that has become an exile and a fugitive from the life led under the Father, knowing not that those who put themselves far from Him shall perish; if he has squandered the gift, and substance, and inheritance of the Father; if there is one whose faith has failed, and whose hope is spent, by rushing along with the Gentiles into the same profligacy of debauchery; and then, famished and destitute, and not even filled with what the swine eat, has arisen and come to his Father!!

But the kind Father waits not till the son comes to Him. For perchance he would never be able or venture to approach, did he not find Him gracious. Wherefore, when he merely wishing, when he straightway made a beginning, when he took the first step, while he was yet a great way off, He [the Father] was moved with compassion, and ran, and fell upon his neck and kissed him. And then the son, taking courage, confessed what he had done.

Wherefore the Father bestows on him the glory and honour that was due and meet, putting on him the best robe, the robe of immortality; and a ring, a royal signet and divine seal,—impress of consecration, signature of glory, pledge of testimony (for it is said, "He hath set to his seal that God is true," John iii. 33); and shoes, not those perishable ones which he that hath set his foot on holy ground is bidden take off, nor such as he who is sent to preach the kingdom of heaven is forbidden to put on, but such as wear not, and are suited for the journey to heaven, becoming and adorning the heavenly path, such as unwashed feet never put on, but those which are washed by our Teacher and Lord.

Many, truly, are the shoes of the sinful soul, by which it is bound and cramped. For each man is cramped by the cords of his own sins. Accordingly, Abraham swears to the king of Sodom, "I will not take of all that is thine, from a thread to a shoe-latchet" (Gen. xiv. 23). On account of these being defiled and polluted on the earth, every kind of wrong and selfishness engrosses life. As the Lord reproves Israel by Amos, saying, "For three iniquities of Israel, yea, for four, I will not turn him back; because they have given away the righteous for silver, and the needy for a pair of shoes, which tread upon the dust of the ground" (Amos ii. 6).

2. Now the shoes which the Father bids the servant give to the repentant son who has betaken himself to Him, do not impede or drag to the earth (for the earthly tabernacle weighs down the anxious mind); but they are buoyant, and ascending, and waft to heaven, and serve as such a ladder and chariot as he requires who has turned his mind towards the Father. For, beautiful after being first beautifully adorned with all these things without, he enters into the gladness within. For "Bring out" was said by Him who had first said, "While he was yet a great way off, he ran and fell upon his neck." For it is here[1] that all the preparation for entrance to the marriage to which we are invited must be accomplished. He, then, who has been made ready to enter will say, "This my joy is fulfilled" (John iii. 29). But the unlovely and unsightly man will hear, "Friend, how camest thou in here, without having a wedding garment?" (Matt. xxii. 12.) And the fat and unctuous food,—the delicacies abundant and sufficing of the blessed,—the fatted calf is killed; which is also again spoken of as a lamb (not literally);

---

[1] We have ventured to substitute ἐνταῦθα instead of ἐντεῦθεν. He is showing that the preparation must be made before we go in.

that no one may suppose it small; but it is the great and greatest. For not small is "the Lamb of God who taketh away the sin of the world" (John i. 29), who "was led as a sheep to the slaughter," the sacrifice full of marrow, all whose fat, according to the sacred law, was the Lord's. For He was wholly devoted and consecrated to the Lord; so well grown, and to such excessive size, as to reach and extend over all, and to fill those who eat Him and feed upon Him. For He is both flesh and bread, and has given Himself as both to us to be eaten.

To the sons, then, who come to Him, the Father gives the calf, and it is slain and eaten. But those who do not come to Him He pursues and disinherits, and is found to be a most powerful bull. Here, by reason of His size and prowess, it is said of Him, "His glory is as that of an unicorn" (Num. xxiii. 22). And the prophet Habakkuk sees Him bearing horns, and celebrates His defensive attitude—"horns in His hands" (Hab. iii. 4). Wherefore the sign shows His power and authority,—horns that pierce on both sides, or rather, on all sides, and through everything. And those who eat are so strengthened, and retain such strength from the life-giving food in them, that they themselves are stronger than their enemies, and are all but armed with the horns of a bull; as it is said, "In thee shall we butt our enemies" (Ps. xliv. 5).

3. Gladness there is, and music, and dances; although the elder son, who had ever been with and ever obedient to the Father, takes it ill, when he who never had himself been dissipated or profligate sees the guilty one made happy.

Accordingly the Father calls him, saying, "Son, thou art ever with me." And what greater joy and feast and festivity can be than being continually with God, standing by His side and serving Him? "And all that is mine is thine." And blessed is the heir of God, for whom the Father holds possession,—the faithful, to whom the whole world of possessions belongs.

"It was meet that we should be glad, and rejoice; for thy brother was dead, and is alive again." Kind Father, who givest all things life, and raisest the dead. "And was lost, and is found." And "blessed is the man whom Thou hast chosen and accepted" (Ps. lxiv. 4), and whom having sought, Thou dost find. "Blessed are those whose iniquities are forgiven, whose sins are covered" (Ps. xxxii. 1). It is for man to repent of sins; but let this be accompanied with a change that will not be checked. For he who does not act so shall be put to shame, because he has acted not with his whole heart, but in haste.

And it is ours to flee to God. And let us endeavour after this ceaselessly and energetically. For He says, "Come unto me, all ye that labour and are heavy laden, and I will give you rest" (Matt. xi. 28). And prayer and confession with humility are voluntary acts. Wherefore it is enjoined, "First tell thy sins, that thou mayest be justified" (Isa. xliii. 26). What afterwards we shall obtain, and what we shall be, it is not for us to judge.

4. Such is the strict meaning of the parable.[1]

The repentant son came to the pitying Father, never hoping for these things,—the best robe, and the ring, and the shoes, —or to taste the fatted calf, or to share in gladness, or enjoy music and dances; but he would have been contented with obtaining what in his own estimation he deemed himself worth. "Make me," he had made up his mind to say, "as one of thy hired servants." But when he saw the Father's welcome meeting him, he did not say this, but said what he had in his mind to say first, "Father, I have sinned against Heaven, and before thee." And so both his humility and his accusation became the cause of justification and glory. For the righteous man condemns himself in his first words. So also the publican departed justified rather than the Pharisee. The son, then, knew not either what he was to obtain, or how to take or use or put on himself the things given him; since he did not take the robe himself, and put it on. But it is said, "Put it on him." He did not himself put the ring on his

---

[1] Here Grabe notes that what follows is a new exposition of the parable, and is by another and a later hand, as is shown by the refutation of Novatus towards the end.

finger, but those who were bidden "Put a ring on his hand." Nor did he put the shoes on himself, but it was they who heard, "and shoes on his feet."

And these things were perhaps incredible to him and to others, and unexpected before they took place; but gladly received and praised were the gifts with which he was presented.

5. The parable exhibits this thought, that the exercise of the faculty of reason has been accorded to each man. Wherefore the prodigal is introduced, demanding from his father his portion, that is, of the state of mind, endowed by reason. For the possession of reason is granted to all, in order to the pursuit of what is good, and the avoidance of what is bad. But many who are furnished by God with this make a bad use of the knowledge that has been given them, and land in the profligacy of evil practices, and wickedly waste the substance of reason,—the eye on disgraceful sights, the tongue on blasphemous words, the smell on fœtid licentious excesses of pleasures, the mouth on swinish gluttony, the hands on thefts, the feet on running into plots, the thoughts on impious counsels, the inclinations on indulgence on the love of ease, the mind on brutish pastime. They preserve nothing of the substance of reason unsquandered. Such an one, therefore, Christ represents in the parable, — as a rational creature, with his reason darkened, and asking from the Divine Being what is suitable to reason; then as obtaining from God, and making a wicked use of what had been given, and especially of the benefits of baptism, which had been vouchsafed to him; whence also He calls him a prodigal; and then, after the dissipation of what had been given him, and again his restoration by repentance, [He represents] the love of God shown to him.

6. For He says, " Bring hither the fatted calf, kill it, and let us eat and be merry; for this my son "—a name of nearest relationship, and significative of what is given to the faithful —"was dead and lost,"—an expression of extremest alienation; for what is more alien to the living than the lost and dead? For neither can be possessed any more. But having

from the nearest relationship fallen to extremest alienation, again by repentance he returned to near relationship. For it is said, " Put on him the best robe," which was his the moment he obtained baptism. I mean the glory of baptism, the remission of sins, and the communication of the other blessings, which he obtained immediately he had touched the font.

"And put a ring on his hand." Here is the mystery of the Trinity; which is the seal impressed on those who believe.

"And put shoes on his feet," for " the preparation of the gospel of peace " (Eph. vi. 15), and the whole course that leads to good actions.

7. But whom Christ finds lost, after sin committed since baptism, those Novatus, enemy of God, resigns to destruction. Do not let us then reckon any fault if we repent; guarding against falling, let us, if we have fallen, retrace our steps. And while dreading to offend, let us, after offending, avoid despair, and be eager to be confirmed; and on sinking, let us haste to rise up again. Let us obey the Lord, who calls to us, " Come unto me, all ye that labour, and I will give you rest" (Matt. xi. 28). Let us employ the gift of reason for actions of prudence. Let us learn now abstinence from what is wicked, that we may not be forced to learn in the future. Let us employ life as a training school for what is good; and let us be roused to the hatred of sin. Let us bear about a deep love for the Creator; let us cleave to Him with our whole heart; let us not wickedly waste the substance of reason, like the prodigal. Let us obtain the joy laid up, in which Paul exulting, exclaimed, " Who shall separate us from the love of Christ?" (Rom. viii. 35.) To Him belongs glory and honour, with the Father and the Holy Spirit, world without end. Amen.

IN MACARIUS CHRYSOCEPHALUS' ORAT. VIII. ON MATT. VIII., AND BOOK VII. ON LUKE XIII.

Therefore God does not here take the semblance of man, but of a dove, because He wished to show the simplicity and gentleness of the new manifestation of the Spirit by the likeness of the dove. For the law was stern, and punished with the sword; but grace is joyous, and trains by the word of meekness. Hence the Lord also says to the apostles, who said that He should punish with fire those who would not receive Him, after the manner of Elias: "Ye know not what manner of spirit ye are of" (Luke ix. 55).

FROM THE SAME.—BOOK XIII. CHAP. IX.

Possibly by the "iota and the tittle" His righteousness exclaims, "If ye come right to me, I also will come right to you; if ye walk crooked, I also will walk crooked, saith the Lord of hosts" (Lev. xxvi. 24), alluding to the offences of sinners under the name of crooked ways. For the straight way, and that according to nature, which is pointed out by the iota of Jesus, is His goodness, which is immoveable towards those who have obediently believed. There shall not then pass away from the law neither the iota nor the tittle; that is, neither the promise that applies to the straight in the way, nor the punishment threatened against those that diverge. For the Lord is good to the straight in the way; but "those that turn aside after their crooked ways He shall lead forth with those that work iniquity" (Ps. cxxv. 5). "And with the innocent He is innocent, and with the froward He is froward" (Ps. xviii. 27); and to the crooked He sends crooked ways.

His own luminous image God impressed as with a seal, even the greatest,—on man made in His likeness, that he might be ruler and lord over all things, and that all things might serve him. Wherefore God judges man to be wholly His, and His own image. He is invisible; but His image, man, is visible. Whatever one, then, does to man, whether good or bad, is referred to Himself. Wherefore from Him judgment shall proceed, appointing to all according to desert; for He will avenge His own image.

(XII.)

FRAGMENTS NOT GIVEN IN THE OXFORD EDITION.

IN ANASTASIUS SINAITA, QUEST. 96.

As it is possible even now for man to form men, according to the original formation of Adam, He no longer now creates, on account of His having granted once for all to man the power of generating men, saying to our nature, "Increase, and multiply, and replenish the earth" (Gen. i. 28). So also, by His omnipotent and omniscient power, He arranged that the dissolution and death of our bodies should be effected by a natural sequence and order, through the change of their elements, in accordance with His divine knowledge and comprehension.

JOANNES VECCUS, PATRIARCH OF CONSTANTINOPLE, ON THE PROCESSION OF THE SPIRIT. IN LEO ALLATIUS, VOL. I. P. 248.

Further, Clement the Stromatist, in the various definitions which he framed, that they might guide the man desirous of studying theology in every dogma of religion, defining what spirit is, and how it is called spirit, says: "Spirit is a substance, subtle, immaterial, and which issues forth without form."

FROM THE UNPUBLISHED DISPUTATION AGAINST ICONOCLASTS, OF NICEPHORUS OF CONSTANTINOPLE; EDITED IN GREEK AND LATIN BY LE NOURRY IN HIS APPARATUS TO THE LIBRARY OF THE FATHERS, VOL. I. P. 1334 A.B. FROM CLEMENT THE PRESBYTER OF ALEXANDRIA'S BOOK AGAINST JUDAIZERS.

Solomon the son of David, in the books styled "The Reigns of the Kings," comprehending not only that the structure of the true temple was celestial and spiritual, but had also a reference to the flesh, which He who was both the son and Lord of David was to build up, both for His own presence, where, as a living image, He resolved to make His shrine, and for the church that was to rise up through the union of faith, says expressly, " Will God in very deed dwell with men on the earth ?" (1 Kings viii. 27.)

He dwells on the earth clothed in flesh, and His abode with men is effected by the conjunction and harmony which obtains among the righteous, and which build and rear a new temple. For the righteous are the earth, being still encompassed with the earth; and earth, too, in comparison with the greatness of the Lord. Thus also the blessed Peter hesitates not to say, " Ye also, as living stones, are built up, a spiritual house, a holy temple, to offer up spiritual sacrifices, acceptable to God by Jesus Christ" (1 Pet. ii. 5).

And with reference to the body, which by circumscription He consecrated as a hallowed place for Himself upon earth, He said, " Destroy this temple, and in three days I will raise it up again. The Jews therefore said, In forty-six years was this temple built, and wilt thou raise it up in three days? But He spake of the temple of His body" (John ii. 19-21).

FROM MS. MARKED 2431 IN THE LIBRARY OF THE MOST CHRISTIAN KING.—IBID. P. 1336 A. FROM THE VERY HOLY AND BLESSED CLEMENT, PRESBYTER OF ALEXANDRIA, THE STROMATIST'S BOOK ON PROVIDENCE.

What is God? " God," as the Lord saith, " is a Spirit." Now spirit is properly substance, incorporeal, and uncircumscribed. And that is incorporeal which does not consist of a body, or whose existence is not according to breadth, length, and depth. And that is uncircumscribed[1] which has

---

[1] With an exclamation of surprise at the Latin translator giving a translation which is utterly unintelligible, Capperonn amends the text, substituting οὗ τόπος οὐδεὶς τῷ, etc., for οὐ τόπος οὐδεὶς τόπος τὸ, etc., and translates accordingly. The emendation is adopted, with the exception of the τῷ, instead of which τό is retained.

no place, which is wholly in all, and in each entire, and the same in itself.

FROM THE SAME MS.—IBID. 1885 D.

Φύσις (nature) is so called from τὸ πεφυκέναι (to be born). The first substance is everything which subsists by itself, as a stone is called a substance. The second is a substance capable of increase, as a plant grows and decays. The third is animated and sentient substance, as animal, horse. The fourth is animate, sentient, rational substance, as man. Wherefore each one of us is made as consisting of all, having an immaterial soul and a mind, which is the image of God.

IN JOHN OF DAMASCUS—PARALLEL.—VOL. II. P. 307.

The fear of God, who is impassable, is free of perturbation. For it is not God that one dreads, but the falling away from God. He who dreads this, dreads falling into what is evil, and dreads what is evil. And he that fears a fall wishes himself to be immortal and passionless.

THE SAME, P. 341.

Let there be a law against those who dare to look at things sacred and divine irreverently, and in a way unworthy of God, to inflict on them the punishment of blindness.

THE SAME, P. 657.

Universally, the Christian is friendly to solitude, and quiet, and tranquillity, and peace.

FROM THE CATENA ON THE PENTATEUCH, PUBLISHED IN LATIN BY FRANCIS ZEPHYRUS, P. 146.

That mystic name which is called the Tetragrammaton, by which alone they who had access to the Holy of Holies were protected, is pronounced Jehovah, which means, "Who is, and who shall be." The candlestick which stood at the south of the altar signified the seven planets, which seem to us to revolve around the meridian,[1] on either side of which rise three branches; since the sun also, like the lamp, balanced in the midst of the planets by divine wisdom, illumines by its light those above and below. On the other side of the altar was situated the table on which the loaves were displayed, because from that quarter of the heaven vital and nourishing breezes blow.

FROM J. A. CRAMER'S CATENÆ GRÆCORUM PATRUM IN NOV. TEST. OXFORD 1840, VOL. III.

On Acts vii. 24, 25. The mystics say that it was by his word alone that Moses slew the Egyptian; as certainly afterwards it is related in the Acts that [Peter] slew with his word those who kept back part of the price of the land, and lied.

THE SAME, VOL. IV. P. 291.

On Rom. viii. 38. "Or life, that of our present existence," and "death,"—that caused by the assault of persecutors, and "angels, and principalities, and powers," apostate spirits.

P. 869, CHAP. X. 3.

And having neither known nor done the requirement of the law, what they conceived, that they also thought that the law required. And they did not believe the law, as prophesying, but the bare word; and followed it from fear, but not with their disposition and in faith.

VOL. VI. P. 385.

On 2 Cor. v. 16. "And if we have known Christ after the flesh."

And so far, he says, no one any longer lives after the flesh. For that is not life, but death. For Christ also, that

---

[1] See Miscellanies, Book v. chap. vi. p. 241, Ante-Nicene Library. which is plainly the source from which this extract is taken.

He might show this,[1] ceased to live after the flesh. How? Not by putting off the body! Far be it! For with it as His own He shall come, the Judge of all. But by divesting Himself of physical affections, such as hunger, and thirst, and sleep, and weariness. For now He has a body incapable of suffering and of injury.

As "after the flesh" in our case is being in the midst of sins, and being out of them to be "not after the flesh;" so also after the flesh, in the case of Christ, was His subjection to natural affections, and not to be subject to them was not to be "after the flesh." "But," he says, "as He was released, so also are we."[2] Let there be no longer, he says, subjection to the influences of the flesh. Thus Clement, the fourth book of the *Hypotyposes*.

FROM THE SAME, P. 391.

On 2 Cor. vi. 11. "Our heart is enlarged."

For as heat is wont to expand, so also love. For love is a thing of warmth. As if he would say, I love you not only with mouth, but with heart, and have you all within. Wherefore he says: "Ye are not straitened in us, since desire itself expands the soul." "Our heart is enlarged" to teach you all things; "but ye are straitened in your own bowels," that is, in love to God, in which you ought to love me.

Thus Clement, in the fourth book of the *Hypotyposes*.

FROM VOL. VII. P. 286.

Heb. i. 1. "At sundry times and divers manners."

Since the Lord, being the Apostle of the Almighty, was sent to the Hebrews, it was out of modesty that Paul did not

---

[1] We omit ὅτι, which the text has after διείξῃ, which seems to indicate the omission of a clause, but as it stands is superfluous. The Latin translator retains it; and according to his rendering, the translation would be, "showed that He ceased."

[2] This extract, down to "are we," has already been given among the extracts from the *Hypotyposes*, p. 158.

subscribe himself apostle of the Hebrews, from reverence for the Lord, and because he was the herald and apostle of the Gentiles, and wrote the Epistle to the Hebrews in addition [to his proper work].[1]

The same work contains a passage from *The Instructor*, book i. chap. vi. (Ante-Nicene Library, Clem. Alex. vol. i.) The passage is that beginning, "For the blood is found to be," etc., p. 140, down to "potent charms of affection," p. 146.

Portions, however, are omitted. There are a good many various readings; but although the passage in question, as found in Cramer's work, is printed in full in Migne's edition, on the alleged ground of the considerable variation from the text of Clement, the variation is not such as to make a translation of the passage as found in Cramer of any special interest or value.

We have noted the following readings:

γίνεται, in p. 141, where, the verb being omitted, we have inserted *is*: There is an obstruction, etc.

σύριγγας, tubes, instead of σήραγγας (hollows), hollows of the breasts.

γειτνιαζουσῶν, for γειτνιουσῶν, neighbouring (arteries).

ἐπιλήψει, for ἐμπεριλήψει, interruption (such as this).

ἀποκλήρωσις occurs as in the text, for which the emendation ἀπολήρησις, as specified in the note, has been adopted.

ἥτις ἐστί, omitted here, which is "sweet through grace," is supplied.

P. 142.

γάλα, milk, instead of μάννα, manna, (that food) manna.

P. 143.

χρὴ δὲ κατανοῆσαι τὴν φύσιν (but it is necessary to consider nature), for οὐ κατανενοηκότες, τ. φ., through want of consideration of nature.

---

[1] This extract, almost verbatim, has been already given from Eusebius, among the extracts from the *Hypotyposes*, p. 161.

κατακλειομένη, agreeing with food, for κατακλειομένῳ, agreeing with heat (enclosed within).

γίνεται for γὰρ (which is untranslated), (the blood) is (a preparation) for milk.

P. 144.

τοίνυν τὸν λόγον is supplied, and εἰκότως omitted in the clause, Paul using appropriate figurative language.

P. 145.

πλὴν is supplied before ἀλλὰ τὸ ἐν αὐτῇ, and the blood in it, etc., is omitted.

P. 146.

"For Diogenes Apolloniates will have it" is omitted.

πάντη, rendered "in all respects," is connected with the preceding sentence.

P. 147.

ὅτι τοίνυν, for 'Ὡς δ'. And that (milk is produced).

τηνικαῦτα for τηνικάδε in the clause, "and the grass and meadows are juicy and moist," not translated.

προειρημένῳ, above mentioned (milk), omitted.

τρυφῆς for τροφῆς, (sweet) nutriment.

τῷ omitted before γλυκεῖ, sweet (wine), and καθάπερ, "as, when suffering."

τὸ λιπαρὸν for τῷ λιπαρῷ, and ἀριδήλως for ἀριδήλου, in the sentence: "Further, many use the fat of milk, called butter, for the lamp, plainly," etc.

INDEXES.

I.—INDEX OF TEXTS OF SCRIPTURE.

OLD TESTAMENT.

GENESIS.

	PAGE
i. 1,	117
i. 2,	118
i. 3,	129
xiv. 23,	169

LEVITICUS.

xxvi. 24,	174

NUMBERS.

xxiii. 22,	170

DEUTERONOMY.

xvii. 16,	121

1 KINGS.

viii. 27,	176

JOB.

i. 21,	154
xxiv. 7,	156

PSALMS.

xviii. 1,	132
xviii. 26,	129
xviii. 27,	174
xviii. 43,	130
xviii. 50,	130
xix. 1,	131
xix. 2, 3,	132
xix. 8,	134
xix. 12,	135
xxxii. 1,	171
xliv. 5,	170
lxiv. 4,	171
cxxv. 4,	157
cxxv. 5,	174

PROVERBS.

xiii. 24,	118

ISAIAH.

ii. 3,	134
xix. 20,	121

	PAGE
xl. 6,	120
xliv. 6,	129

HOSEA.

i. 2,	117
i. 7,	118
i. 10, 11,	118
v. 2,	118
v. 8,	118

AMOS.

ii. 6,	169

HABAKKUK.

iii. 4,	170

APOCRYPHA.
WISDOM.

iii. 7,	129

NEW TESTAMENT.

MATTHEW.

iii. 11,	124
iii. 12,	124
v. 6,	121
v. 42,	156
vi. 9,	142
vi. 27,	120
vi. 33, 32,	120
xi. 28,	171, 173
xii. 44,	120
xii. 46,	157
xii. 50,	123
xiii. 31, 32,	156
xiii. 43,	133
xxii. 12,	169
xxiii. 9,	123
xxvi. 17,	167

LUKE.

i. 43,	131
iii. 22,	157, 174
ix. 55,	120
xii. 25,	120

	PAGE
xii. 49,	125
xv. 11, etc.,	168, etc.
xvi. 17,	157
xxiv. 34,	130

JOHN.

i. 29,	170
iii. 3,	168
iii. 29,	169
xvi. 7,	140

ACTS.

vii. 24, 25,	178

ROMANS.

viii. 15,	122
viii. 35,	173
viii. 38,	178

1 CORINTHIANS.

i. 18,	126
v. 5,	142
xi. 10,	158
xv. 49,	124

EPHESIANS.

vi. 15,	173

1 TIMOTHY.

ii. 6,	160
iii. 16,	160
v. 8,	160
v. 10,	161
v. 21,	161
vi. 13,	161

2 TIMOTHY.

ii. 2,	161

HEBREWS.

i. 1,	143, 179

1 PETER.

i. 3,	139
i. 10,	140

	PAGE		PAGE		PAGE
i. 12,	140	iii. 22,	142	iii. 1, 2,	151
i. 19,	141	iv. 5,	142	iii. 8–10, 15, 16, 20,	
i. 20,	141	iv. 13,	143	21, 24,	152
i. 23,	141	iv. 17,	143	iv. 18,	152
i. 25,	141	v. 10,	143	iv. 24,	176
ii. 5,	140, 176	v. 14,	143	v. 6, 7, 14, 19, 20,	153
ii. 9,	141				
ii. 23,	141	1 JOHN.		2 JOHN.	
iii. 10,	141	i. 1,	147	Ver. 10,	153
iii. 12,	142	i. 2, 5, 7, 10,	148		
iii. 15,	142	ii. 1–3,	149	JUDE.	
iii. 18,	142	ii. 5, 7–14,	150	Ver. 1, 4, 5, 6, 7, 8,	144
iii. 20,	142	ii. 16, 17, 19, 22, 23,		Ver. 9, 10, 11, 12,	
iii. 21,	142	29,	151	13, 14, 19,	146

II.—INDEX OF PRINCIPAL SUBJECTS.

ABORTIONS, committed to guardian angels, 130.
Above all rule and authority, 134.
Abysses, the, 117.
Achilles, 99.
Adæus, St., and St. Maris, Liturgy composed by, 77, etc.
Advocate with the Father, the, 149.
Afflictions of the righteous, the object of, 119.
Agamemnon, 98.
Alms, 156.
Ambrose, the conversion of, 97.
Angels, guardian, of exposed infants, 129; guardians of abortives, 130; who preside over generation, 131; first created, 131; set over the stars, 132; men changed into, 134; those called spirits of Christ, 140; desire to look into divine things, 140; subject to Christ, 142; that kept not their pre-eminence, 144; effect divine operations, and influenced the prophets, 149; veiled on account of, 158; saw Christ, 160.
Apostles, the baptism of, 159.
Apostles, the Liturgy of, 73, etc.; another, 77, etc.
Athlete, the, 126.

BAPTISM, 118, 119; with fire, 124; of the apostles, 159; the "best robe" put on in, 173; repentance of sin after, 173.
Beginning, 118, 147.
Being, 162.

CÆSAR, rendering to, what is his, 123.
Calmness, 156.
Care, worldly, to be avoided, 120.
"Chains of darkness," 144.
Cherubic hymn, the, 19.
Christ, knowing Him after the flesh, 178, 179.
Contentment inculcated, 109, 110.
Crabs, what they represent, 164, 165.
Cross, signing with the sign of, in prayer, instances of, 23, 28, 38, 56, 57, 63, 76, 78, 85, 86, 87, 88, 90.
Crucifixion of the flesh, the, 158.

DEAD, the gospel preached to the, 142.
Delusion, the, which has its abode in the world, 108, 109.
Devil, the, his knowledge and ignorance in relation to our Lord, 132.
Dove, the descent of a, on Jesus, 157, 173.
Dreamers, 144.

ELECT, the, and the lost, 151.
Electa, 153.
"Eli, Eli," 134, and *note*.

FASTING, 121.
Fathers, young men, and children, 150.
Fatted calf, the, 169, 170.
Faults, secret, 135.
Fear and love, 122, 123.
Fear of God, 177.
Festivals, heathen, 103, 104.
Fire, baptism with, 124; God a con-

suming, 124, 125; Christ came to send, on earth, 125.
Firmament, the, 131, 132.
Flattery, 155, 156.
Flesh, crucifying the, 158; living after the, 178, 179.

GOD, the soul to be filled with, 120; employs the agency of men for effecting good, 121; the power of, 121, 122; the worthiness of, incomprehensible, 123; a consuming fire, 124, 125; is light and love, 148; no darkness in, *ibid.*; a spirit, 176.
Gospels, the order of the composition of, 162.

HEARTS, enlarged, 179.
Heavens, the, 131.
Hebrews, the Epistle to the, translated by Luke out of Hebrew, 160; why Paul did not affix his name to, 160, 162.
Hector, 98.
Helen, 98.
Hephæstus and Venus, 101.
Homer, his gods and heroes, 98, 99.
Horns, their emblematic import, 170.
House, the, swept and empty, 120.
House, a spiritual, 140.

IMAGE of God, man made in the, 174.
Incarnation, the, 123.
Incense, prayers at the offering of, 12, 13, 19, 50, 53, 56, 61, 80, 85.
Infant, the complaint of a, on entering the world, 154, 155.
Infants, exposed and abortive, cared for by angels, 129, 130.
Iota and tittle, 157, 174.

JAMES the Just, 159; anecdote of, 161.
James, the Liturgy of, 11, etc.
Jehovah, 177.
Jesus, the baptism of, 119; descent of a dove on, 157, 173.
John, comments on the first Epistle of, 147, etc.; second Epistle of, 153; character of the Gospel of, 162.
Jude, author of the Catholic Epistle so called, 143; comments on the Epistle of, 144.
Jupiter, his character and deeds, 144.

KISSING the altar, 84; the host, 86.
Knowledge, 120, 126, 128.
Kora, 100, 101.

Kronos devours his children, 102.

LAW of the Lord, the, 134.
Learning to be preferred to riches, 109.
Liberty, 122, 123.
Life, the sadness and misery of, 155.
Life and good days, 141.
Light, God is, 148.
Light and darkness, 150.
Liturgies, primitive, an account of, 3, etc.
Longsuffering, 130.
Love, 179.
Love, God is, 148.
Love and fear, 122.
Luke and his writings, 143.

MARA, a letter of, to Serapion, 105, etc.; the laughter of, 114.
Mark, how and when he composed his Gospel, 143, 159, 162.
Mark, the Liturgy of, 47.
Medea, 103.
Men, some, changed into angels, 134.
Milk of women, curious statements respecting, 130, 131.
Moses slaying the Egyptian, 178.
Mustard-seed, the parable of the grain of, 156.

NAKED from the earth, and naked returning to the earth, 154.
Nakedness of man by nature, the advantages arising from, 155.
Nature, 162.

ODYSSEUS, 98, 99.
Œdipus, 103.

PASSIONS of the soul, 130.
Passover, the, 167.
Paul, why he did not affix his name to the Epistle to the Hebrews, 160, 162, 179, 180.
Pearl of great price, the, 157.
Penelope, 101.
Peter, the relation of, to the Gospel of Mark; discrepant statements respecting, 159, 160.
Pluto carries off Kora, 100, 101.
Power of God, the, 121, 122.
Prayer, the power of, 121.
Pre-existence, the, of man denied, 122.
Priesthood, a royal, 141.
Procne, and her sister, 103, *note.*
Prodigal son, the parable of, 168–173.
Property, we are not bidden to renounce, 130.

Prophecy, Pantænus' remarks on the use of the tenses in, 133.
Propitiation, the prayer of, 45.

REASON, man naturally endowed with, and may abuse, 172.
Regeneration, 118, 139.
Repentance, 164; of sin after baptism, 173.
Resurrection, the, 139.
Riches, learning to be preferred to, 109; the love of, disturbs life, 110; men intent on possessing, 112.
Right hand of God, the, 146.
Robe, the best, and the ring, 168, 172.

SCRIPTURES, the use of, 126; to be searched diligently, 127.
Sedrach, Misak, and Abednago, the song of, 117.
Shoes, the, given to the returned prodigal, 168, 169.
Sin after baptism may be repented of, 173.
Slander, 164.
Sodom and Gomorrah, 144.
Sons of God, 151.
Soul, the, to be filled with God, 120; not naturally immortal, 140; corruptible, 141; all souls immortal, 163.
Speaking and writing compared, 125.
Spirit, 175, 176.
Stars, the, 132.
Stars, wandering, 145.
Substance, 177.

Sufferings, feeling among the ancients in respect to personal, 119, 120; of Christ, partakers of the, 143.
Sun, how God sets His tabernacle in the, 132, 133, 134; an angel in, rules the day, 133.

TEMPLE, the, of Solomon a type, 175, 176.
Tenses, the use of the, in prophecy, 133.
Tetragrammaton, the, 177.
Three, the, which bear witness, 153.
Thrones, principalities, etc., 134.
Thyestes, 103.
"Trees, autumnal, without fruit," 145.
Trisagion hymn, 15; prayer, 52.
Trojan war, the, 98.

UNCLEAN spirit's return, the, 120.
Ungodly men, the, described and denounced by Jude, 145.

VEIL, prayer of the, 26.
Venus, Hephæstus, and Ares, 101.

WATER, the, above the firmament, 119.
"Waves of a raging sea," 145.
Willing, 163.
Wise, the persecutors of the, punished, 110.
Witnesses, two or three, 121.
Writing and speaking compared, 125.
Word, the, 147; handling of, *ibid.*

THE END.

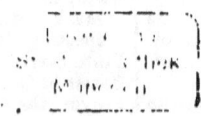

MURRAY AND GIBB, EDINBURGH,
PRINTERS TO HER MAJESTY'S STATIONERY OFFICE.

T. and T. Clark's Publications.

In Four Handsome Volumes, 8vo, price 32s.,
The Comparative Geography of Palestine and the Sinaitic
Peninsula. By Professor CARL RITTER of Berlin. Translated and adapted for the use of Biblical Students by WILLIAM L. GAGE.

'To clergymen these volumes will prove not less interesting than instructive and useful. Theological students will find in them the most exhaustive storehouse of facts on the subjects existing in the language, while upon all the moot points of Palestinian and Sinaitic geography they will meet with a condensed summary of all the arguments of every writer of note, from the earliest ages down to the period of the author's death. In a word, these four volumes give the essence of the entire literature of the subject of every age and language. . . . . The readers of these volumes have every reason to be satisfied with the result. . . . . But it would be impossible to mention all the good things in these volumes. We must, however, say a few words upon Ritter's magnificent monograph on the situation of Ophir, which we regard as one of the gems of the work. . . . . Ritter's treatment of this apparently hopeless question is a masterpiece of mature scholarship and sound judgment. The whole monograph is a model of its kind. . . . . What we are now saying of the monograph on the situation of Ophir is, however, applicable to everything our author wrote.'—*Spectator*.

'It is superfluous to commend such a peerless work as this.'—*British Quarterly Review*.

In 8vo, price 10s. 6d.,
Commentary on the Greek Text of the Epistle of Paul to the
Galatians. By Rev. JOHN EADIE, D.D., LL.D., Professor of Biblical Literature and Exegesis to the United Presbyterian Church.

'A full and elaborate commentary on the Epistle to the Galatians. Dr. Eadie has had no common task before him, but he has done the work remarkably well.'—*Contemporary Review*.

'The volume as a whole is a most valuable addition to the theological literature of Scotland, in that department in which it is of much consequence that it should receive additions. It has confirmed Dr. Eadie's claim to a high place among British expositors.'—*United Presbyterian Magazine*.

In One Volume, demy 8vo, price 10s. 6d.,
Analytical Commentary on the Epistle to the Romans, tracing
the Train of Thought by the aid of Parallelism; with Notes and Dissertations on the Principal Difficulties in the Epistle. By JOHN FORBES, LL.D., Professor of Oriental Languages, Aberdeen University.

'Dr. Forbes' Commentary takes a far wider and deeper range than any merely external rule of interpretation, and it is marked by good sense and able reasoning.'—*Guardian*.

'In every point of view it is a valuable addition to critical biblical literature, and possesses many attractions even for the unlearned reader. For full satisfaction on every difficulty we have referred with complete satisfaction to this modest yet learned and exhaustive work.'—*Contemporary Review*.

In crown 8vo, price 3s. 6d.,
Evangelical Meditations. By Professor Vinet.
'The work before us is one which will be most highly prized by the spiritually-minded and single-hearted Christian.'—*Patriot*.

In post 8vo, price 3s. 6d., Second Edition,
Pastoral Theology: The Theory of a Gospel Ministry. By
Professor VINET.

'One or two rapid readings will not suffice to exhaust the treasures of Christian and pastoral experience, of enlightenment, of tenderness, of practical directions, of elevation, and of edification, which fill these pages. We will find it to our profit to read at least once a year this precious volume, if it were only as the means of serving as pastors for the examination of our conscience.'—*Archives du Christianisme*.

In demy 8vo, price 9s., Second Edition,
Homiletics; or, The Theory of Preaching. By Professor Vinet.
'Vinet, from his previous studies, was especially at home on such a subject, in which he finds scope, not only for his powers of exposition, but also for his rich faculty of criticism, some exquisite gems of which are scattered up and down its pages.'—*North British Review*.

T. and T. Clark's Publications.

In post 8vo, price 2s.,

Vital Christianity: Essays and Discourses on the Religions of
Man and the Religion of God. By Professor VINET.

In crown 8vo, price 4s. 6d., Sixth Edition,

The Suffering Saviour; or, Meditations on the Last Days of
the Sufferings of Christ. By Dr. F. W. KRUMMACHER.

'We give it preference to everything hitherto produced by the gifted and devoted author. It is divinity of the most thoroughly evangelical description. Truth and tenderness have seldom been so successfully combined. A book of the heart, to *that* it appeals in every page, with a force which it will be difficult to resist.'—*Christian Witness.*

One Volume, crown 8vo, price 5s., Cheap Edition,

Gotthold's Emblems; or, Invisible Things understood by
Things that are Made. By CHRISTIAN SCRIVER, Minister of Magdeburg in 1671. Translated from the Twenty-eighth German Edition.

'A peculiarly fascinating volume. It is rich in happy and beautiful thoughts, which grow on the root of genuine piety.'—*Witness.*

In crown 8vo, price 5s., Third Edition,

Light from the Cross: Sermons on the Passion of our Lord.
Translated from the German of A. THOLUCK, D.D., Professor of Theology in the University of Halle, by the Rev. R. C. LUNDIN BROWN, M.A.

'With no ordinary confidence and pleasure we commend these most noble, solemnizing, and touching discourses.'—*British and Foreign Evangelical Review.*

In One Thick Volume, 8vo, price 9s.,

Greek and English Lexicon of the New Testament. By
EDWARD ROBINSON, D.D., late Professor Extraordinary of Sacred Literature in the Theological Seminary, Andover. A New and Improved Edition, revised by ALEXANDER NEGRIS, Professor of Greek Literature, and by the Rev. JOHN DUNCAN, D.D., Professor of Oriental Languages in the New College, Edinburgh.

In Two Volumes, crown 8vo, price 10s. 6d.,

Modern Pantheism: Essay on Religious Philosophy. By
M. EMILE SAISSET, Professor of the History of Philosophy in the Faculty of Letters in Paris. Translated from the French. With Marginal Analysis, Notes, Critical Essay, and Philosophical Appendix. The original draft of this work obtained the prize offered by the Academy of Moral and Political Sciences on the following subject: *Examen Critique des Principaux Systèmes Modernes de Theodicée.* The second edition carried off the first of the great Monthyon Prizes of the French Academy.

'As a handbook to the theological side of modern speculation, it is a most valuable addition to philosophical literature. The translation is clear and idiomatic; it is English in its language, French in the transparency of its expression.'—*Saturday Review.*

Just published, in crown 8vo, price 6s., Third Edition,

The Tripartite Nature of Man, Spirit, Soul, and Body, applied
to Illustrate and Explain the Doctrines of Original Sin, the New Birth, the Disembodied State, and the Spiritual Body. By Rev. G. B. HEARD, M.A. With an Appendix on the Fatherhood of God.

'The author has got a striking and consistent theory. Whether agreeing or disagreeing with that theory, it is a book which any student of the Bible may read with pleasure.' —*Guardian.*

This day is published, in demy 8vo, price 9s.,

Sermons. From 1828 to 1860. By the late William Cunningham,
D.D., Principal and Professor of Church History, New College, Edinburgh. With Photograph. Edited, with a Preface, by Rev. J. J. BONAR, Greenock.

T. and T. Clark's Publications.

Just published, in demy 8vo, Second Edition, price 10s. 6d.,

The Doctrine of the Atonement, as Taught by Christ Himself;
or, The Sayings of Jesus on the Atonement Exegetically Expounded and Classified. By GEORGE SMEATON, D.D., Professor of Exegetical Theology, New College, Edinburgh.

'We attach very great value to this seasonable and scholarly production. The idea of the work is most happy, and the execution of it worthy of the idea. On a scheme of truly Baconian exegetical induction, he presents us with a complete view of the various positions or propositions which a full and sound doctrine of the atonement embraces.'—*British and Foreign Evangelical Review*.

'The plan of the book is admirable. A monograph and exegesis of our Lord's own sayings on this greatest of subjects concerning Himself must needs be valuable to all theologians. And the execution is thorough and painstaking—exhaustive, as far as the completeness of range over these sayings is concerned.'—*Contemporary Review*.

Just published, in demy 8vo, price 10s. 6d.,

The Doctrine of the Atonement, as Taught by the Apostles;
or, The Sayings of the Apostles Exegetically Expounded. By GEORGE SMEATON, D.D., Professor of Exegetical Theology, New College, Edinburgh.

'We cannot too highly commend the conception and general execution of this really great theological work. Professor Smeaton may claim the honour of having inaugurated, at any rate in Scotland, a *novum organum* of theology. . . . His book is a great and noble work—a credit to British biblical scholarship, and a great service to doctrinal theology.' —*British Quarterly Review*.

Lately published, in One Volume, crown 8vo, price 5s.,

Rome and the Council in the Nineteenth Century. Translated
from the French of FELIX BUNGENER, with additions by the Author.

'The present volume is admirable for its brief, compact, trenchant logic; for its comprehensiveness of range; for its profound and searching criticism of the principles and developments of Popery. . . . It is a searching, eloquent, and in every way remarkable volume.'—*London Quarterly Review*.

In demy 8vo, price 9s.,

The Old Catholic Church; or, The History, Doctrine, Worship,
and Polity of the Christians, traced from the Apostolic Age to the Establishment of the Pope as a Temporal Sovereign, A.D. 755. By W. D. KILLEN, D.D., Belfast.

'This valuable work embraces about one half of the interval between the birth of Christ and the Reformation. The author has bestowed much pains in consulting authorities, has condensed the history very carefully, and has written with much clearness and vivacity. . . . . We recommend Dr. Killen's work as a very admirable and useful compendium of the ecclesiastical period of which he treats.'—*Evangelical Magazine*.

In Three Volumes, royal 8vo, price 36s.,

History of the Christian Church. By Philip Schaff, D.D., Author
of 'The History of the Apostolic Church.' From the Birth of Christ to Gregory the Great, A.D. 1-600.

'Dr. Schaff's book is perhaps, taken all in all, the most convenient, serviceable, and satisfactory of all our general Church histories, especially for students.'—*Presbyterian*.

'Dr. Schaff's "Church History," for working purposes, is by far the best we possess. . . . . We would gladly have devoted to a work so thorough, scholarly, catholic, and able, a lengthened review.'—*British Quarterly Review*.

In Two Volumes, 8vo, price 21s.,

The Church of Christ: A Treatise on the Nature, Powers,
Ordinances, Discipline, and Government of the Christian Church. By the late JAMES BANNERMAN, D.D., Professor of Apologetics and Pastoral Theology, New College, Edinburgh. Edited by his Son.

'The general tone of the work is dignified, earnest, temperate, and devout. We heartily recommend it to the shelves of our universities and students of theology.'—*London Quarterly Review*.

T. and T. Clark's Publications.

In One Volume, demy 8vo, price 9s.,

Discourses on Redemption; as Revealed at 'Sundry Times and in Divers Manners,' through Patriarchs, Prophets, Jesus, and His Apostles. By S. ROBINSON, D.D.

'One of those works a clergyman will most highly prize, inasmuch as there is a mine of suggestive writing to be found in it which may be worked with profit for many a day.'—*Ecclesiastical Gazette.*

In One Volume, crown 8vo, price 6s.,

Friedrich Wilhelm Krummacher: an Autobiography. Edited by his Daughter, and Translated by Rev. M. G. EASTON, M.A. Second Edition, revised, with a new Biographical Supplement by the Editor.

'Dr. Krummacher of Potsdam, so well known by his "Elisha" and "Elijah" and "David," died on the 10th of December last. Among his papers was found an autobiography extending down to the year 1848. This autobiography, with a portrait and various additions bringing it down to the day of his death, has now been published, and we are sure that all who know anything of its subject—and who does not?—will eagerly secure the book, and not lay it down till they have finished it.'—*Bibliotheca Sacra.*

Just published, in One Handsome Volume, demy 8vo, price 10s. 6d.,

The Training of the Twelve; or, An Exposition of Passages in the Gospels exhibiting the Twelve Disciples of Jesus under Discipline for the Apostleship. By the Rev. ALEXANDER BALMAIN BRUCE.

'Here we have a really great book on an important, large, and attractive subject; and it must be a matter of congratulation among all theological renders, that a subject so important has fallen into the hands of one thoroughly qualified to do it justice. Certainly we can name no work either in our own or any other language, in which we find a clearer conception of the principles of the Christian religion, and of the adaptation of these to all that is deepest in human nature. . . . It is one of those rare books which ring in our ears as the utterance of a true man, who speaks because his heart and mind are free.'—*British and Foreign Evangelical Review.*

Just published, in One Volume, handsomely bound, crown 8vo, price 7s. 6d.,

The Footsteps of Christ. Translated from the German of A. CASPERS by A. E. RODHAM. 1. Christ for us; 2. Christ in us; 3. Christ before us; 4. Christ through us.

'It is a work of solid thought and solid learning, and should find a considerable public in its English dress.'—*Nonconformist.*

'The sentences are short and antithetical, and the translation is so idiomatic and good, that you never have occasion in reading to notice that it is a translation at all. The papers are short, but not too short for a profitable devout meditation in the closet. They are admirably fitted for that purpose; indeed, that is their sole aim and end. We close by simply recommending any and every reader, who may be in search of a really fresh devotional volume, to stop here at this one.'—*Weekly Review.*

'The volume is entirely devotional, and contains much that will have interest for devout and intelligent English readers. . . . It ought to find a welcome.'—*Freeman.*

Just published, in Two Volumes, demy 8vo, price 21s.,

Commentary, Exegetical and Critical, on the Acts of the Apostles. By the Rev. PATON GLOAG, D.D., Minister of Blantyre.

'Dr. Gloag's work is very acceptable. . . . The volumes are scholarly, earnest, trustworthy, and supply materials for the refutation of the speculations of the critical school.'—*British Quarterly Review.*

In crown 8vo, Fifth Edition, price 7s. 6d.,

Christ's Second Coming: Will it be Pre-Millennial? By DAVID BROWN, D.D.

'This is, in our judgment, one of the most able, comprehensive, and conclusive of the numerous works which the millenarian controversy has called forth.'—*Watchman.*

In foolscap 8vo, price 5s.,

The Parables of Christ Illustrated and Expounded. By Dr. F. G. LISCO.

T. and T. Clark's Publications.

Just published, in Two Handsome Volumes, 8vo, price 21s.,

History of Protestant Theology, particularly in Germany, viewed according to its Fundamental Movement, and in connection with the Religious, Moral, and Intellectual Life. Translated from the German of Dr. J. A. DORNER, Professor of Theology at Berlin. With a Preface to the Translation by the Author.

'This work, which may be called a History of Modern Theology, is one of the most important, interesting, and useful that Messrs. Clark have ever issued. A careful study of it would systematise on the reader's mind the whole round of evangelical truth. In fact it is, in a certain sense, a comprehensive view of Historical Theology written on a new plan; not in the form of the tabulated summary, but as traced in the living history of those whose struggles won for us the truth, and whose science formulated it for posterity.'—*London Quarterly Review.*

Just published, in crown 8vo, Second Edition, price 6s.,

Apologetic Lectures on the Fundamental Truths of Christianity. Second Edition. By Professor LUTHARDT. The Antagonistic Views of the World in their Historical Development; The Anomalies of Existence; The Personal God; The Creation of the World; Man; Religion; Revelation; History of Revelation—Heathenism and Judaism; Christianity in History; The Person of Jesus Christ.

'We have never met with a volume better adapted to set forth the evidences of Christianity in a form suited to the wants of our day. There is no obscurity in the thoughts or in the style; the language is simple, the ideas clear, and the argument logical, and generally, to our mind, conclusive. . . . . The whole of this vast argument is illustrated by various and profound learning in ancient and modern writers, and the notes themselves are an interesting study. We confidently recommend these valuable lectures both to the student and the general reader, as containing an unusual amount of thought and information, conveyed in elegant and forcible language.'—*Guardian.*

In crown 8vo, price 6s.,

Apologetic Lectures on the Saving Truths of Christianity. Second Edition in the Press. By Professor LUTHARDT. The Nature of Christianity; Sin; Grace; The God-Man; The Work of Jesus Christ; The Trinity; The Church; Holy Scripture; The Means of Grace; The Last Things.

'These lectures contain a *resumé* of the doctrines of the Christian faith. The author is a profound thinker, a skilled theologian, a man of wide and varied culture, who knows how to express clearly and sharply what he believes. The principles of the gospel are expounded with singular force, truth, and gracefulness of diction.'—*Evangelical Magazine.*

Just published, in crown 8vo, price 4s. 6d.,

The Problem of Evil. By Ernest Naville, late Professor of Philosophy, University of Geneva. Translated from the French by E. W. SHALDERS, B.A. 1. Good; 2. Evil; 3. The Problem; 4. The Solution; 5. The Proof; 6. The Battle of Life; 7. Succour.

'This most difficult subject is handled with a power and mastery as rare as delightful, and with a substantial orthodoxy not always to be looked for under philosophical forms and methods. The book is of remarkable weight and power. . . . . We give it our warmest recommendation.'—*Literary Churchman.*

'The book is a good philosophical defence of what theologically is the doctrine of original sin, and it defends its thesis throughout with a studied absence of all theological language or argument by purely philosophical reasoning.'—*Guardian.*

In demy 8vo, price 7s. 6d.,

The Religions before Christ: Being an Introduction to the History of the First Three Centuries of the Church. By E. DE PRESSENSE, D.D.

'Stamped with the true genius of a historian, and imbued with the devoutness of a Christian.'—*Patriot.*

T. and T. Clark's Publications.

In crown 8vo, price 6s.,

The Redeemer. Discourses by E. de Pressense, D.D. With Introduction by W. LINDSAY ALEXANDER, D.D.

'The whole volume is marked by a rare richness of thought and illustration, and by a high and fervid eloquence.'—*Evangelical Magazine.*

In Two Volumes, demy 8vo, price 21s.,

Mediatorial Sovereignty: The Mystery of Christ and the Revelation of the Old and New Testaments. By GEORGE STEWARD.

'A large and exhaustive work, with great fulness of argument.'—*Christian Remembrancer.*

'Certainly one of the books of the age,—we might say of the century. Anything more massive, comprehensive, and thoroughly theological, we cannot name. The author has achieved a noble triumph on behalf of the cause he loves.'—*Christian Witness.*

In demy 8vo, price 9s.,

The Scripture Testimony to the Holy Spirit. By James MORGAN, D.D., Belfast.

'Controversy and criticism are avoided. Scripture ideas are unfolded in a clear and popular way, so as not only to inform the judgment, but also to purify the heart.'—*Evangelical Magazine.*

In demy 8vo, price 9s.,

An Exposition of the First Epistle of St. John. By James MORGAN, D.D., Belfast.

In Two Volumes, crown 8vo, price 12s.,

Biblical Studies on St. John's Gospel. By Dr. Besser.

'We now call attention to the great merits of this volume. The character of this commentary is practical and devotional. There are often very exquisite devotional passages, and a vein of earnest piety runs through the whole work. We recommend the book most warmly to all.'—*Literary Churchman.*

'There is a quiet, simple, penetrating good sense in what Dr. Besser says, and withal a spirit of truly Christian devoutness, which the reader must feel to be in beautiful accordance with the inspired teachings which awaken it.'—*British Quarterly Review.*

In Two Volumes, 8vo, price 21s.,

A History of Christian Doctrine. By W. G. Shedd, Professor of Theology, Union College, New York.

'We do not hesitate to pronounce the work a great improvement on anything we have had before. To the young student it will be valuable as a guide to his critical reading, and to the literary man it will be indispensable as a book of reference.'—*Bibliotheca Sacra.*

In demy 8vo, price 10s. 6d.,

A Critical and Exegetical Commentary on the Book of Genesis. With a new Translation. By JAMES G. MURPHY, LL.D., T.C.D.

'Dr. Murphy has conferred a great service on a difficult department of scriptural learning.'—*Clerical Journal.*

In demy 8vo, price 9s.,

A Critical and Exegetical Commentary on the Book of Exodus. By JAMES G. MURPHY, LL.D., T.C.D.

In demy 8vo, price 10s. 6d.,

The Early Scottish Church. The Ecclesiastical History of Scotland, from the First to the Middle of the Twelfth Century. By T. M'LAUCHLAN, D.D., LL.D., Edinburgh.

In crown 8vo, price 5s.,

The Sinlessness of Jesus: An Evidence for Christianity. By Dr. C. ULLMANN.

'We warmly recommend this beautiful work as eminently fitted to diffuse among those who peruse it a higher appreciation of the sinlessness and moral eminence of Christ.'—*British and Foreign Evangelical Review.*

CLARK'S
FOREIGN THEOLOGICAL LIBRARY.

ANNUAL SUBSCRIPTION:
One Guinea (payable in advance) for Four Volumes, Demy 8vo.
When not paid in advance, the Retail Bookseller is entitled to charge 24s.

N.B.—Any two Years in this Series can be had at Subscription Price. A single Year's Books (except in the case of the current Year) cannot be supplied separately. Non-subscribers, price 10s. 6d. each volume, with exceptions marked.

1864—
Lange on the Acts of the Apostles. Two Volumes.
Keil and Delitzsch on the Pentateuch. Vols. I. and II.

1865—
Keil and Delitzsch on the Pentateuch. Volume III.
Hengstenberg on the Gospel of John. Two Volumes.
Keil and Delitzsch on Joshua, Judges, and Ruth. One Volume.

1866—
Keil and Delitzsch on Samuel. One Volume.
Keil and Delitzsch on Job. Two Volumes.
Martensen's System of Christian Doctrine. One Volume.

1867—
Delitzsch on Isaiah. Vol. I.
Delitzsch on Biblical Psychology. 12s.
Delitzsch on Isaiah. Vol. II.
Auberlen on Divine Revelation.

1868—
Keil's Commentary on the Minor Prophets. Two Volumes.
Delitzsch's Commentary on Epistle to the Hebrews. Vol. I.
Harless' System of Christian Ethics. One Volume.

1869—
Hengstenberg on Ezekiel. One Volume.
Stier on the Words of the Apostles. One Volume.
Keil's Introduction to the Old Testament. Vol. I.
Bleek's Introduction to the New Testament. Vol. I.

1870—
Keil's Introduction to the Old Testament. Vol. II.
Bleek's Introduction to the New Testament. Vol. II.
Schmid's New Testament Theology. One Volume.
Delitzsch's Commentary on Epistle to the Hebrews. Vol. II.

1871—
Delitzsch's Commentary on the Psalms. Vols. I. and II.
Hengstenberg's History of the Kingdom of God under the Old Testament. Vol. I.
Delitzsch's Commentary on the Psalms. Vol. III.

1872—
Keil's Commentary on the Books of Kings. One Volume. } *First*
Keil's Commentary on the Book of Daniel. One Volume. } *Issue.*

MESSRS. CLARK have resolved to allow a SELECTION of TWENTY VOLUMES (*or more at the same ratio*) from the various Series previous to the Volumes issued in 1868 (*see next page*),

At the Subscription Price of Five Guineas.

They trust that this will still more largely extend the usefulness of the FOREIGN THEOLOGICAL LIBRARY, which has so long been recognised as holding an important place in modern Theological literature.

T. and T. Clark's Publications.

CLARK'S FOREIGN THEOLOGICAL LIBRARY—*Continued.*

The following are the works from which a Selection may be made (non-subscription prices within brackets):—

Dr. E. W. Hengstenberg.—**Commentary on the Psalms.** By E. W. HENGSTENBERG, D.D., Professor of Theology in Berlin. In Three Volumes 8vo. (33s.)

Dr. J. C. L. Gieseler.—**Compendium of Ecclesiastical History.** By J. C. L. GIESELER, D.D., Professor of Theology in Göttingen. Five Volumes 8vo. (£2, 12s. 6d.)

Dr. Hermann Olshausen.—**Biblical Commentary on the Gospels and Acts,** adapted especially for Preachers and Students. By HERMANN OLSHAUSEN, D.D., Professor of Theology in the University of Erlangen. In Four Volumes demy 8vo. (£2, 2s.)

Biblical Commentary on the Romans, adapted especially for Preachers and Students. By HERMANN OLSHAUSEN, D.D., Professor of Theology in the University of Erlangen. In One Volume 8vo. (10s. 6d.)

Biblical Commentary on St. Paul's First and Second Epistles to the Corinthians. By HERMANN OLSHAUSEN, D.D., Professor of Theology in the University of Erlangen. In One Volume 8vo. (9s.)

Biblical Commentary on St. Paul's Epistles to the Galatians, Ephesians, Colossians, and Thessalonians. By HERMANN OLSHAUSEN, D.D., Professor of Theology in the University of Erlangen. In One Volume 8vo. (10s. 6d.)

Biblical Commentary on St. Paul's Epistle to the Philippians, to Titus, and the First to Timothy; in continuation of the Work of Olshausen. By LIC. AUGUST WIESINGER. In One Volume 8vo. (10s. 6d.)

Biblical Commentary on the Hebrews. By Dr. EBRARD. In continuation of the Work of Olshausen. In One Volume 8vo. (10s. 6d.)

Dr. Augustus Neander.—**General History of the Christian Religion and Church.** By AUGUSTUS NEANDER, D.D. Translated from the Second and Improved Edition. In Nine Volumes 8vo. (£2, 11s. 6d.)
This is the only Edition in a Library size.

Prof. H. A. Ch. Havernick.—**General Introduction to the Old Testament.** By Professor HAVERNICK. One Volume 8vo. (10s. 6d.)

Dr. Ju ius Müller.—**The Christian Doctrine of Sin.** B Dr. JULIUS MÜLLER. Two Volumes 8vo. (21s.) New Edition.

Dr. E. W. Hengstenberg.—**Christology of the Old Testament, and a Commentary on the Messianic Predictions.** By E. W. HENGSTENBERG, D.D., Professor of Theology, Berlin. Four Volumes. (£2, 2s.)

Dr. M. Baumgarten.—**The Acts of the Apostles; or the History of the Church in the Apostolic Age.** By M. BAUMGARTEN, Ph.D., and Professor in the University of Rostock. Three Volumes. (£1, 7s.)

Dr. Rudolph Stier.—**The Words of the Lord Jesus.** By RUDOLPH STIER, D.D., Chief Pastor and Superintendent of Schkeuditz. In Eight Volumes 8vo. (£4, 4s.)

Dr. Carl Ullmann.—**Reformers before the Reformation,** principally in Germany and the Netherlands. Translated by the Rev. R. MENZIES. Two Volumes 8vo. (£1, 1s.)

Professor Kurtz.—**History of the Old Covenant; or, Old Testament Dispensation.** By Professor KURTZ of Dorpat. In Three Volumes. (£1, 11s. 6d.)

Dr. Rudolph Stier.—**The Words of the Risen Saviour, and Commentary on the Epistle of St. James.** By RUDOLPH STIER, D.D., Chief Pastor and Superintendent of Schkeuditz. One Volume. (10s. 6d.)

Professor Tholuck.—**Commentary on the Gospel of St. John.** By Professor THOLUCK of Halle. In One Volume. (9s.)

Professor Tholuck.—**Commentary on the Sermon on the Mount.** By Professor THOLUCK of Halle. In One Volume. (10s. 6d.)

Dr. E. W. Hengstenberg.—**Commentary on the Book of Ecclesiastes.** To which are appended: Treatises on the Song of Solomon; on the Book of Job; on the Prophet Isaiah; on the Sacrifices of Holy Scripture; and on the Jews and the Christian Church. By E. W. HENGSTENBERG, D.D. In One Volume 8vo. (9s.)

T. and T. Clark's Publications.

CLARK'S FOREIGN THEOLOGICAL LIBRARY—Continued.

Dr. John H. A. Ebrard.—Commentary on the Epistles of St. John. By Dr. JOHN H. A. EBRARD, Professor of Theology in the University of Erlangen. In One Volume. (10s. 6d.)

Dr. J. P. Lange.—Theological and Homiletical Commentary on the Gospel of St. Matthew and Mark. Specially Designed and Adapted for the Use of Ministers and Students. By J. P. LANGE, D.D., Professor of Divinity in the University of Bonn. Three Volumes. (10s. 6d. each.)

Dr. J. A. Dorner.—History of the Development of the Doctrine of the Person of Christ. By Dr. J. A. DORNER, Professor of Theology in the University of Berlin. Five Volumes. (£2, 12s. 6d.)

Lange and Dr. J. J. Van Oosterzee.—Theological and Homiletical Commentary on the Gospel of St. Luke. Specially Designed and Adapted for the Use of Ministers and Students. Edited by J. P. LANGE, D.D. Two Volumes. (18s.)

Professor Kurtz.—The Sacrificial Worship of the Old Testament. One Volume. (10s. 6d.)

Professor Ebrard.—The Gospel History: A Compendium of Critical Investigations in support of the Historical Character of the Four Gospels. One Volume. (10s. 6d.)

Lange, Lechler, and Gerok.—Theological and Homiletical Commentary on the Acts of the Apostles. Edited by Dr. LANGE. Two Volumes. (21s.)

Dr. Hengstenberg.—Commentary on the Gospel of St. John. Two Volumes. (21s.)

Professor Keil.—Biblical Commentary on the Pentateuch. Three Volumes. (31s. 6d.)

Professor Keil.—Commentary on Joshua, Judges, and Ruth. One Volume. (10s. 6d.)

Professor Delitzsch.—A System of Biblical Psychology. One Volume. (12s.)

Professor Delitzsch.—Commentary on the Prophecies of Isaiah. Two Volumes. (21s.)

Professor Auberlen.—The Divine Revelation: An Essay in Defence of the Faith. One Volume. (10s. 6d.)

Professor Keil.—Commentary on the Books of Samuel. One Volume. (10s. 6d.)

Professor Delitzsch.—Commentary on the Book of Job. Two Volumes. (21s.)

Bishop Martensen.—Christian Dogmatics. A Compendium of the Doctrines of Christianity. One Volume. (10s. 6d.)

Dr. J. P. Lange.—Critical, Doctrinal, and Homiletical Commentary on the Gospel of St. John. Two Volumes. (21s.)

And, in connection with the Series,—

Ritter's (Carl) Comparative Geography of Palestine. Four Volumes. (32s.)
Shedd's History of Christian Doctrine. Two Volumes. (21s.)
Macdonald's Introduction to the Pentateuch. Two Volumes. (21s.)
Hengstenberg's Egypt and the Books of Moses. (7s. 6d.)
Ackerman on the Christian Element in Plato. (7s. 6d.)
Robinson's Greek Lexicon of the New Testament. 8vo. (9s.)
Gerlach's Commentary on the Pentateuch. Demy 8vo. (10s. 6d.)

The above, in 116 Volumes (including 1872), price £30, 9s., form an *Apparatus*, without which it may be truly said *no Theological Library can be complete;* and the Publishers take the liberty of suggesting that no more appropriate gift could be presented to a Clergyman than the Series, in whole or in part.

⁎⁎ *In reference to the above, it must be noted that* NO DUPLICATES *can be included in the Selection of Twenty Volumes; and it will save trouble and correspondence if it be distinctly understood that* NO LESS *number than Twenty can be supplied, unless at non-subscription price.*

Subscribers' Names received by all Retail Booksellers.

CHEQUES on COUNTRY BANKS under £2, 2s. must have 6d. added for Bank charge.

LONDON: (*For Works at Non-subscription price only*) HAMILTON, ADAMS, & CO.

T. and T. Clark's Publications.

CHEAP RE-ISSUE
OF THE WHOLE
WORKS OF DR. JOHN OWEN.
Edited by Rev. W. H. GOOLD, D.D., Edinburgh.
WITH LIFE BY REV. ANDREW THOMSON, D.D.

In 24 Volumes, demy 8vo, handsomely bound in cloth, lettered.

With Two Portraits of Dr. Owen.

Several years have now elapsed since the first publication of this edition of the Works of the greatest of Puritan Divines. Time has tested its merits; and it is now admitted on all hands to be the only correct and complete edition.

At the time of publication it was considered—as it really was—a miracle of cheapness, having been issued, by Subscription, for Five Guineas.

In consequence of the abolition of the Paper Duty, the Publishers now re-issue the Twenty-four Volumes for

FOUR GUINEAS.

As there are above Fourteen Thousand Pages in all, each Volume therefore averages *Five Hundred and Ninety Pages.*

'You will find that in John Owen the learning of Lightfoot, the strength of Charnock, the analysis of Howe, the savour of Leighton, the raciness of Heywood, the glow of Baxter, the copiousness of Barrow, the splendour of Bates, are all combined.' We should quickly restore the race of great divines if our candidates were disciplined in such lore.'—*The Late* Dr. HAMILTON *of Leeds.*

CONTENTS.

VOLS.
- I. Life, by Rev. Dr. Thomson; Christologia, or a Declaration of the glorious Mystery of the Person of Christ; Meditations on the Glory of Christ; Two Short Catechisms.
- II. Of Communion with God the Father, Son, and Holy Ghost.
- III. and IV. On the Holy Spirit.
- V. On the Doctrine of Justification by Faith.
- VI. Of the Mortification of Sin in Believers; the Nature, Power, etc., of the Remainders of Sin in Believers; Practical Exposition of the cxxx. Psalm.
- VII. Nature and Causes of Apostasy from the Gospel; the Grace and Duty of being Spiritually Minded; of the Dominion of Sin and Grace.
- VIII. and IX. Sermons.
- X. A Display of Arminianism; the Death of Death in the Death of Christ; of the Death of Christ; Dissertation on Divine Justice.
- XI. Doctrine of the Saints' Perseverance explained.
- XII. Mystery of the Gospel vindicated and Socinianism examined.
- XIII. Duty of Pastors and People distinguished; Eshcol; of Schism, etc.
- XIV. On a Treatise, 'Fiat Lux;' the Church of Rome no Safe Guide, etc.
- XV. Discourse concerning Liturgies and their Imposition; concerning Evangelical Love, Church Peace and Unity; Inquiry into the Original, Nature, Institution, Power, Order, and Communion of Evangelical Churches, etc.
- XVI. The True Nature of a Gospel Church, etc.; Three Treatises concerning the Scriptures.
- XVII. Theologumena, sive de natura, ortu, progressu, et studio veræ Theologiæ.
- XVIII. to XXIV. Exposition of the Epistle to the Hebrews.

₊ *Separate Volumes may be had, price* 8s. 6d. *each.*

T. and T. Clark's Publications.

(TEMPORARY) CHEAP RE-ISSUE

OF

STIER'S WORDS OF THE LORD JESUS.

To meet a very general desire that the now well-known Work of Dr. STIER,

THE WORDS OF THE LORD JESUS,

should be brought more within the reach of all classes, both Clergy and Laity, Messrs. CLARK have resolved to issue the *Eight* Volumes, handsomely bound in *Four*, for

TWO GUINEAS.

This can be only offered for a limited period; and as the allowance to the trade must necessarily be small, orders sent either direct, or through booksellers, must in every case be accompanied with a Post Office Order for the above amount.

'We know no work that contains, within anything like the same compass, so many pregnant instances of what true genius under chastened submission to the control of a sound philology, and gratefully accepting the seasonable and suitable helps of a wholesome erudition, is capable of doing in the spiritual exegesis of the sacred volume. Every page is fretted and studded with lines and forms of the most alluring beauty. At every step the reader is constrained to pause and ponder, lest he should overlook one or other of the many precious blossoms that, in the most dazzling profusion, are scattered around his path. We venture to predict that his *Words of Jesus* are destined to produce a great and happy revolution in the interpretation of the New Testament in this country.'—*British and Foreign Evangelical Review.*

T. and T. Clark's Publications.

The Works of St. Augustine.
EDITED BY THE REV. MARCUS DODS, M.A.

MESSRS. CLARK have much pleasure in publishing the second issue of Translations of the Writings of St. AUGUSTINE—viz.:

WRITINGS IN CONNECTION WITH THE DONATIST CONTROVERSY. One Volume.

THE ANTI-PELAGIAN WORKS OF ST. AUGUSTINE. Vol. I.

The first issue comprised

THE 'CITY OF GOD,'
IN TWO VOLUMES.
Translated by the Rev. Marcus Dods, M.A.

They believe this will prove not the least valuable of their various Series, and no pains will be spared to make it so. The Editor has secured a most competent staff of Translators, and every care is being taken to secure not only accuracy, but elegance.

The Works of St. AUGUSTINE to be included in the Series are (in addition to the 'CITY OF GOD')—

> All the TREATISES in the PELAGIAN, and the four leading TREATISES in the DONATIST CONTROVERSY.
> The TREATISES against FAUSTUS the Manichæan; on CHRISTIAN DOCTRINE; the TRINITY; the HARMONY OF THE EVANGELISTS; the SERMON ON THE MOUNT.
> Also, the LECTURES on the GOSPEL OF ST. JOHN, the CONFESSIONS, a SELECTION from the LETTERS, the RETRACTATIONS, the SOLILOQUIES, and SELECTIONS from the PRACTICAL TREATISES.

All these works are of first-rate importance, and only a small proportion of them have yet appeared in an English dress. The SERMONS and the COMMENTARIES ON THE PSALMS having been already given by the Oxford Translators, it is not intended, at least in the first instance, to publish them.

The Series will include a LIFE OF ST. AUGUSTINE, by ROBERT RAINY, D.D., Professor of Church History, New College, Edinburgh.

The Series will probably extend to Sixteen or Eighteen Volumes. The Publishers will be glad to receive the *Names* of Subscribers as early as possible.

SUBSCRIPTION: Four Volumes for a Guinea, *payable in advance*, as in the case of the ANTE-NICENE SERIES (24s. when not paid in advance).

It is understood that Subscribers are bound to take at least the books of the first two years. Each Volume will be sold separately at (on an average) 10s. 6d. each Volume.

They trust the Subscribers to the ANTE-NICENE LIBRARY will continue their Subscription to this Series, and they hope to be favoured with an early remittance of the Subscription.

T. and T. Clark's Publications.

THE CUNNINGHAM LECTURES.

SECOND SERIES.
In demy 8vo, price 10s. 6d.,

THE DOCTRINE OF JUSTIFICATION:

AN OUTLINE OF ITS HISTORY IN THE CHURCH, AND OF ITS EXPOSITION FROM SCRIPTURE, WITH SPECIAL REFERENCE TO RECENT ATTACKS ON THE THEOLOGY OF THE REFORMATION.

BY JAMES BUCHANAN, D.D.,
PROFESSOR OF DIVINITY, NEW COLLEGE, EDINBURGH.

'Our readers will find in them an able, clear, and comprehensive statement of the truth which forms the subject, clothed in language "suitable alike to an academic and to a popular audience." We only add, that the copious notes and references, after the manner of the Bampton and Hulsean Lectures, beside which it is worthy to stand, greatly enhance the value of the volume, and constitute it a capital handbook of the doctrine of justification.'—*Weekly Review.*

THIRD SERIES.
In demy 8vo, price 10s. 6d.,

THE REVELATION OF LAW IN SCRIPTURE:

CONSIDERED WITH RESPECT BOTH TO ITS OWN NATURE, AND TO ITS RELATIVE PLACE IN SUCCESSIVE DISPENSATIONS.

BY PATRICK FAIRBAIRN, D.D.,
AUTHOR OF 'TYPOLOGY OF SCRIPTURE,' ETC.

'A volume which, independently of his other works, would, in our judgment, suffice to secure for Dr. Fairbairn a place amongst the ablest and soundest of the theologians of the present century. And we have no hesitation in expressing our conviction that the Third Series of the "Cunningham Lectures" has not detracted from the reputation of a community which can exhibit names so illustrious as those which adorn the annals of the Free Church of Scotland.'—*Christian Observer.*

FOURTH SERIES.
This day, in One Vol. demy 8vo, price 6s.,

THEOLOGY AND THEOLOGIANS OF SCOTLAND:

PRINCIPALLY OF THE 17TH AND 18TH CENTURIES.

BY J. WALKER, D.D., CARNWATH.

T. and T. Clark's Publications.

New and Cheaper Edition of Lange's Life of Christ.

Now complete, in Four Volumes, demy 8vo, price 28s. (Subscription price),

THE LIFE OF THE LORD JESUS CHRIST:

A COMPLETE CRITICAL EXAMINATION OF THE ORIGIN, CONTENTS, AND CONNECTION OF THE GOSPELS.

Translated from the German of

J. P. LANGE, D.D.,

PROFESSOR OF DIVINITY IN THE UNIVERSITY OF BONN.

EDITED, WITH ADDITIONAL NOTES,

BY THE REV. MARCUS DODS, M.A.

※ *This valuable Work has been out of print for some time, but has been much in demand. The Six Volumes now occupy Four; and whilst the whole matter is retained, it is published at a little cheaper price.*

Extract from Editor's Preface.

'The work of Dr. Lange, translated in the accompanying volumes, holds among books the honourable position of being the most complete Life of our Lord. There are other works which more thoroughly investigate the authenticity of the Gospel records, some which more satisfactorily discuss the chronological difficulties involved in this most important of histories, and some which present a more formal and elaborate exegetical treatment of the sources; but there is no single work in which all these branches are so fully attended to, or in which so much matter bearing on the main subject is brought together, or in which so many points are elucidated. The immediate object of this comprehensive and masterly work was to refute those views of the life of our Lord which had been propagated by Negative Criticism, and to substitute that authentic and consistent history which a truly scientific and enlightened criticism educes from the Gospels.'

www.ingramcontent.com/pod-product-compliance
Lightning Source LLC
Chambersburg PA
CBHW020906230426
43666CB00008B/1332